The Self-Made Founder: Starting Strong, Scaling Fast

Opening Chapter: The Founder's Awakening

1. **Chapter 1: The Mindset Shift – The Foundation of a Self-Made Founder**
   Why start here? This chapter is your launchpad. It focuses on the most important element of any journey—the mind. The foundation of your startup begins with your personal evolution. A compelling narrative and thought-provoking questions that make the reader stop and reflect on their current mindset.
   "If you're not ready to change the way you think, you're not ready to be a founder."

Part 1: Building from the Inside Out – Crafting Your Identity

2. **Chapter 2: Discovering Your Why – Creating a Purpose-Driven Startup**
   A deep dive into understanding why you're starting this journey. It will inspire the reader to dig into their passions and transform them into

purpose-driven businesses.

"When you know your 'Why', your startup becomes unstoppable."

3. **Chapter 3: Time Management for Founders – Getting Things Done in the Early Stages**
   What does a founder's day really look like? This chapter teaches the art of working smarter, not harder, by building strong time management habits from the start.

   "In the world of startups, time is not money—it's your survival."

4. **Chapter 4: Embracing Failure – Learning From Setbacks and Bouncing Back**
   A non-linear path, this chapter comes early but is essential for growth. Failure is framed as a necessary step in the journey, not a setback.

   "Every failure is a lesson in disguise—if you're brave enough to see it."

Part 2: Taking Action – From Idea to Execution

5. **Chapter 5: Turning Ideas into Action – Moving from Dreamer to Doer**
   Moving from thought to action is the hardest step. This chapter emphasizes how to start turning your ideas into something tangible.
   "The difference between an idea and a business is execution."

6. **Chapter 6: Building Your MVP – From Idea to First Product**
   No fluff. Just actionable steps to build your first MVP. This chapter will challenge readers to stop overthinking and start building.
   "Don't wait for perfect—launch with purpose."

7. **Chapter 7: Finding Product-Market Fit – The Key to Sustainable Growth**
   Product-market fit is the ultimate goal for any startup. This chapter will equip readers with the tools to know when they've hit it, and how to iterate

if they haven't.

"Product-market fit isn't something you find—it's something you create."

8. **Chapter 8: Sales and Customer Acquisition – Turning Leads Into Loyal Customers**
Sales are the lifeblood of any business. This chapter redefines sales for the modern founder—no hard-selling, just meaningful connections.

"Customers don't buy products, they buy solutions."

Part 3: Building Your Empire – Leadership, Networking, and Growth

9. **Chapter 9: Bootstrapping vs. Fundraising – The Right Approach for Your Startup**
A creative approach to both bootstrapping and fundraising, outlining the pros and cons of each option with real-life examples from successful founders.

"Bootstrap like a champion, or raise like a visionary—just choose wisely."

10. **Chapter 10: Building a Lean Team – Hiring Your First Employees or Contractors**
    Growing your team doesn't always mean hiring tons of people. This chapter will show how to start lean and build a team that supports your vision.

    "It's not about how many people you have; it's about the right people in the right places."

11. **Chapter 11: Creating Relationships – Networking and Mentorship for Startup Growth**
    This chapter flips the narrative on networking. It's about building genuine relationships that last, not just making connections for the sake of it.

    "Your net worth is defined by your network—and the value you offer."

12. **Chapter 12: Growth Hacks – Scaling Your Startup Fast with**

Minimal Resources
Resourceful growth strategies that scale businesses quickly, without the big budget. It's about working smarter, not harder.

"When you're scrappy, every small win is a giant leap."

Part 4: Sustainable Success – Keeping Your Startup on Track

13. **Chapter 13: Cash Flow and Budgeting – Keeping Your Startup Financially Healthy**
    A creative twist on financial literacy for founders who hate numbers but need to understand them.

    "Money isn't just the lifeblood of your startup—it's the pulse you need to stay alive."

14. **Chapter 14: Building Your Brand Identity – Creating a Memorable Startup Brand**
    This chapter dives deep into how to build a brand that resonates with your target audience and sticks in

their minds.

"Great businesses aren't built on products—they're built on unforgettable brands."

15. **Chapter 15: Leadership and Team Building – How to Lead During the Growth Phase**

    A creative look at leadership that's human-centered and inspiring. It focuses on how to lead with empathy and authenticity.

    "Leadership isn't about authority—it's about influence."

16. **Chapter 16: The Pivot – When and How to Change Course Without Losing Momentum**

    Not every plan works, and that's okay. This chapter talks about recognizing when a pivot is needed and how to execute it smoothly.

    "Pivots are not failures—they are opportunities in disguise."

Part 5: The Path to Mastery – Scaling for Long-Term Success

17. **Chapter 17: Scaling Your Product – The Art of Expanding Your Offerings**
    Scaling with purpose. How to grow your offerings in a way that aligns with your brand and market demand.
    "Growth isn't about adding more—it's about doing better."

18. **Chapter 18: Future-Proofing Your Business – Building for Long-Term Success**
    The final chapter, which teaches founders to think beyond the now. It's about building systems and diversifying revenue streams that ensure future success.
    "Success is not a destination, it's a journey. Make sure your journey never ends."

Conclusion: From Zero to One and Beyond

- **"Your Next Step"**
  A closing section that urges readers to take action immediately. It emphasizes the importance of moving from theory to execution and

challenges readers to take that first step—right now.

A Letter from Dev Taneja, the Creator of Anime Devta

When I first started my entrepreneurial journey, I had no roadmap, no mentor guiding me, and no solid plan to follow. What I had instead was a vision, a burning desire to create something of my own, and the relentless drive to push forward, even when the path was unclear. I was just an engineering college student trying to navigate the world of business with nothing but a few ideas and a ton of ambition.

Today, Anime Devta is a brand that represents creativity, passion, and the hustle of turning dreams into reality. I'm humbled by the recognition and achievements we've had so far, including being featured as one of the top emerging startups in India by headstart, top 3% under 25 by WTFund led by Nikhil Kamath sir and receiving appreciation and reaching to industry leaders through our products like Aman Gupta - Founder of Boat, Ashneer Grover sir - Founder of Bharat pay, family of Pawan Kalyan sir Deputy CM of Andhra Pradesh, Ranveer Allahbadia and many more. But what I'm most proud of is that **for the past four years**, Anime Devta has been running a **profitable startup in an environment where many others are losing money.**

In a world where many startups struggle to stay afloat, let alone turn a profit, Anime Devta has managed to thrive. I've weathered the ups and downs of the startup ecosystem, from market uncertainties to fierce competition. It wasn't easy, but with a focused mindset, smart decisions, and a strong strategy, we've been able to build a business that not only survives but also grows consistently. This book is a reflection of that journey.

As a founder, you'll encounter more obstacles than you can imagine. It's not about whether you'll face failure—it's about how you'll handle it. And the sooner you realize that every challenge is an opportunity to learn, the faster you'll grow. That's why I decided to write *The Self-Made Founder: Starting Strong, Scaling Fast*. It's not just a business book; it's a guide for the early-stage founders who are still figuring things out. I want to give you the tools, insights, and mindset shifts I wish I had when I first started.

The path from **zero to one**—from an idea to building a thriving business—is one of the toughest, most rewarding journeys you'll ever embark on. I know it because I lived it. But it doesn't have to be as confusing or overwhelming as it often seems. This book is about taking that first step with clarity and confidence. It's about building the right mindset and foundation for success and learning how to scale your business with purpose and speed.

The 18-Month Roadmap to Startup Success

What makes this book unique is that it's not just a theoretical guide—it's a **practical roadmap** designed to take you through the **first 18 months** of your startup journey. These are the critical first 18 months where every decision you make could shape the future of your business.

In each of the **18 chapters**, you'll learn how to approach a different aspect of your business, step-by-step, month by month.

This structure is intentional. Why? Because startups aren't built in a day. It takes time, effort, and strategic decisions to go from ideation to full-scale operation. And most importantly, it's a long game.

Here's how it works:

- **Months 1–6**: These are the critical months where you lay the foundation. You'll focus on discovering your purpose, crafting a powerful vision, and getting clarity on your target market and value proposition.

- **Months 7–12**: Now that your foundation is set, it's time to start building your product, testing your ideas, and launching. You'll face tough decisions about what to prioritize, how to structure your team, and how to start getting customers.

- **Months 13–18**: Once you've made it past your first few product launches and customer experiences, it's time to scale. In this phase, you'll need to master the art of growth, hire the right team, refine your sales processes, and ensure that your business is primed for success.

By breaking down your journey into 18 chapters—one for each month—you'll get clear, actionable steps on what to focus on, what to expect, and how to avoid common pitfalls. Whether you're just starting out or you've been in business for a few months, this roadmap is designed to guide you through the most pivotal phases of your startup journey.

Why This Book? Why Now?

As I reflect on my own journey, I realize that the road to success is often less about intelligence or luck and more about resilience, consistency, and the ability to make decisions based on the best information you have at the moment. Many people want to start something big, but they get stuck in the overwhelming nature of the "how"—How do I start? How do I raise funds? How do I find customers? How do I grow?

I created this book to break those barriers for you. My goal is to offer a no-nonsense guide that helps you move from ideation to execution. Every chapter is designed to help you **start strong** and **scale fast**, so you can confidently build the foundation of a lasting business.

This book is more than just a collection of business strategies—it's a resource for you to build the mindset and the habits you'll need to not only survive in the startup world but thrive in it.

So, whether you're in the early ideation phase or struggling to figure out how to scale, this book will meet you where you are and give you the guidance to keep moving forward.

The journey to success isn't linear, and it isn't easy. But with the right tools and mindset, you can turn your vision into a reality. Let's get started.

- Dev Taneja
Founder, Anime Devta

Chapter 1: The Mindset Shift – The Foundation of a Self-Made Founder

Why Start Here?

Before you build anything—your product, your team, your brand—you must first build *yourself*. No matter how strong your business idea is, your mindset as a founder will be the determining factor between success and failure. It's the invisible hand that shapes every decision, every strategy, and every outcome in your entrepreneurial journey.

This chapter isn't about teaching you to be positive or motivated; it's about giving you the tools to rewire your thinking to handle the unique demands of being a founder. Whether you're working with limited resources, facing rejection, or navigating uncertainty, your ability to think clearly, stay resilient, and adapt is what will carry you forward.

This is your launchpad, the very first building block of your journey. Let's start where it truly matters—*with you*.

The Power of a Founder's Mindset

Think about this: why do two founders with similar ideas, resources, and opportunities achieve completely different outcomes? One thrives while the other barely survives—or worse, gives up entirely. The answer lies in their mindset.

As a founder, you're stepping into a world that demands more from you than any traditional job. You'll face:

- **Uncertainty**: There's no roadmap. You're creating it as you go.
- **Pressure**: Every decision you make impacts not just you, but your team, your customers, and your vision.
- **Loneliness**: The weight of responsibility often rests solely on your shoulders.

To succeed, you need a mindset that can thrive in this chaos—a mindset that doesn't just endure challenges but actively transforms them into opportunities.

Your Mind is the Startup's Operating System

Imagine your startup as a machine. It has moving parts—like your product, team, and marketing strategy—but at its core is the operating system: *you*. If the operating system is weak, the machine can't function properly. Your mindset is that operating system.

Here's the reality:

- **You set the tone for your team**: If you're calm, focused, and optimistic, your team will reflect that. If you're overwhelmed and erratic, so will they be.

- **Your mindset influences decisions**: Fear-based thinking can cause hesitation, while a growth mindset allows you to take calculated risks.

- **You control your resilience**: Challenges are inevitable, but your response to them is entirely in your hands.

A strong, growth-oriented mindset ensures that your "operating system" can handle the pressure, pivot when needed, and keep running even during setbacks.

The Self-Assessment: Where Are You Now?

Before we move forward, take a moment to reflect. Ask yourself:

1. **How do you handle uncertainty?** Do you freeze, overanalyze, or take action?

2. **How do you view failure?** Do you see it as a dead-end or as feedback to improve?

3. **How often do you seek growth?** Are you actively learning, or are you stuck in your comfort zone?

Write down your answers. Be honest. These questions aren't meant to judge you—they're here to help you understand your current mindset. Awareness is the first step toward transformation.

The Two Mindsets: Fixed vs. Growth

Dr. Carol Dweck's research on mindset highlights two contrasting ways of thinking:

1. **Fixed Mindset:**
    - Believes abilities are innate and unchangeable.
    - Avoids challenges for fear of failure.
    - Gives up easily when faced with obstacles.

2. **Growth Mindset:**
    - Believes abilities can be developed through effort.
    - Embraces challenges as opportunities to learn.
    - Perseveres through setbacks and adapts.

As a founder, a growth mindset isn't optional—it's essential. It's what allows you to learn from failures, improve constantly, and innovate even when the odds are against you.

Rewiring Your Mindset: Practical Steps

1. **Shift Your Relationship with Failure**
    - Failure isn't the opposite of success; it's part of the process.
    - View each mistake as a data point—an opportunity to refine your approach.
    - Celebrate your failures as much as your wins because they're signs of progress.

2. **Embrace Uncertainty**
    - Accept that you won't always have the answers—and that's okay.
    - Focus on taking small, consistent actions rather than seeking perfect solutions.

- Remind yourself: uncertainty is where growth happens.

3. **Commit to Lifelong Learning**
    - Devour books, podcasts, and resources on business, leadership, and personal growth.
    - Surround yourself with mentors and peers who challenge your thinking.
    - Stay curious—ask questions, seek feedback, and never stop exploring.

4. **Develop Emotional Resilience**
    - Practice mindfulness or meditation to stay present and manage stress.
    - Cultivate gratitude by reflecting on small wins and progress.
    - Build a support system of people who believe in you and your vision

Thought-Provoking Questions to Ponder

- What's the biggest fear holding you back right now?
- If failure wasn't an option, what would you attempt?
- How do you want to grow—not just as a founder, but as a person?

These aren't just questions; they're seeds. The more you reflect on them, the more they'll shape the way you think, act, and lead.

Recommended Book: Mindset: The New Psychology of Success by Carol S. Dweck

- This book delves into the concepts of a fixed vs. growth mindset and how they impact personal and professional success.

Chapter 2: Discovering Your Why – Creating a Purpose-Driven Startup

Building a startup is an exciting and challenging journey. It's a rollercoaster filled with moments of inspiration, triumphs, setbacks, and uncertainty. Amid this chaos, the one thing that keeps you grounded is your "why." It's your reason for starting, your motivation to keep pushing, and the foundation upon which you'll build your business.

Your "why" is more than a statement—it's your startup's soul. It drives every decision, defines your purpose, and connects you to the people you aim to serve. Without a strong "why," your startup risks becoming just another project that fizzles out when the going gets tough. This chapter is about helping you uncover that core purpose so you can build something that matters—not just to you but to the world.

Why Your Why Matters

When things get hard (and they will), a clear sense of purpose will pull you through. Your "why" keeps you anchored during the late nights, the endless rejections, and the doubts that creep in. But beyond motivation, your "why" is also strategic:

1. **It Differentiates You:** A clear purpose sets you apart in a crowded market. People are drawn to businesses that stand for something.

2. **It Inspires Others:** Customers, employees, and investors don't just buy into your product—they buy into your mission.

3. **It Provides Direction:** When faced with tough decisions, your "why" helps you choose the path that aligns with your core purpose.

Finding Your Why

1. Reflect on Your Core Values

Your "why" begins with what you believe in. Your values act as a compass, guiding your choices and shaping your vision. To uncover these, ask yourself:

- What do I believe the world needs more of?
- What issues or causes do I feel deeply connected to?
- What principles guide my decisions in life and work?

2. Identify Your Passions and Interests

Think about the things that energize you and bring you joy. While passion alone isn't enough to build a business, it's a crucial ingredient for staying engaged over the long term. Consider:

- What do I love doing, even when it's difficult?
- What topics, industries, or ideas do I lose track of time exploring?

3. Look for Problems That Resonate With You

The most successful startups solve problems. Think about challenges you've faced or gaps you've noticed in the world around you. Reflect on:

- What frustrates or annoys me about the status quo?
- What problem would I feel proud to solve, even if it's difficult?

4. Imagine the Impact You Want to Have

Fast-forward 10 or 20 years. Picture the legacy you want to leave behind. Ask yourself:

- How do I want to be remembered?
- What impact do I want my business to have on people's lives or the world?

Crafting Your Why

Your "why" should resonate deeply with you. It's not about impressing others or chasing trends. It's about authenticity. For example:

- A founder creating a health-tech startup might define their "why" as:

"To empower people to take control of their health and live better lives."

- A founder launching a sustainability-focused brand might say:
  "To reduce waste and promote a culture of conscious consumption."

The specifics will vary, but the essence is the same: your "why" is your purpose, distilled into a single, powerful statement.

Connecting Your Why to Your Startup

Once you've uncovered your "why," it's time to tie it to your business vision. This connection is what turns a good idea into a purpose-driven startup. Here's how:

1. **Write a Mission Statement:** Turn your "why" into a clear and actionable mission statement that guides your brand.

2. **Let It Shape Your Brand Identity:** Your "why" should influence your messaging, product design, and customer experience.

3. **Share Your Story:** People love brands with a story. Let your audience know why you do what you do—it will make them care more about your startup.

The Challenges of Defining Your Why

Defining your "why" isn't always easy. It requires self-reflection, vulnerability, and honesty. Sometimes, it's uncomfortable to confront your motivations or admit that your initial ideas might need refinement. But this process is crucial because a shallow or unclear "why" won't sustain you when challenges arise.

It's okay if your "why" evolves over time. Purpose isn't static—it grows as you and your startup grow. The important thing is to start somewhere.

Your Next Step

Take some time to reflect on the exercises in this chapter. Write down your thoughts, even if they feel messy or incomplete. Your "why" doesn't have to be perfect—it just has to feel real to you.

Start with this simple sentence:

- *"I want to build [your startup idea] because [your reason]."*

Keep refining it. Let it evolve as you learn and grow.

Recommended Reading

Start With Why by Simon Sinek
This book dives into the power of purpose and how a clear "why" can inspire both leaders and organizations to succeed. It's an essential read for anyone building a purpose-driven startup.

Chapter 3: Time Management for Founders – Getting Things Done in the Early Stages

As a founder, your time is your most valuable asset. It's easy to get lost in the chaos of building a business, especially in the early stages when you're juggling multiple responsibilities and challenges. You may often feel like there aren't enough hours in the day. But if you can master the art of time management, you can multiply your productivity and make the most of your efforts.

In this chapter, we'll dive deep into how you can manage your time effectively as a founder. I'll share practical advice on how to organize your day, prioritize tasks, and build strong habits that will set you up for long-term success.

Why Time Management Is Critical for Founders

Running a startup is a whirlwind, and in the early stages, everything seems urgent. But urgency doesn't always equal importance.

The way you manage your time—how you allocate your hours, energy, and focus—can make the difference between your business succeeding or failing.

As a founder, you must become the CEO of your time. This means:

1. **Delegating** as much as possible.
2. **Prioritizing** tasks that move the needle.
3. **Building routines** that align with your vision.

Mastering time management will allow you to gain control over your day and maximize your efforts.

Your Time Table – A Template for Success

When I started my journey as a college student, managing my time was crucial for survival. Every day was a battle to fit everything in, but I quickly learned that the key wasn't about working harder, it was about working smarter. It wasn't about achieving the mythical "work-life balance" either—it was about intense focus, being laser-focused on what needed to be done right then and there. I'll share the time table I followed to get things off the ground, but remember, your time table should be personalized to fit your life and goals.

My Time Table as a College Founder

I'll be completely honest here: in the beginning, I had no time for balance, for rest, or even basic self-care. The focus was on creating a successful business. My schedule was packed from morning till night, but it was all driven by purpose. Here's what a typical day looked like for me back when I was starting my business as a college student:

5:00 AM – 6:00 AM: Wake Up

I started my day early, as I found that the quiet hours of the morning were the best for getting a head start on the day. When everyone else was still asleep, I had an edge—free from distractions, I could focus on myself and the tasks at hand.

6:30 AM: Meditation

Meditation was my secret weapon for staying calm in the chaos. It helped me clear my mind and prepare mentally for the challenges ahead. It wasn't long, just 10-20 minutes, but it was a powerful ritual that made me more focused throughout the day.

7:00 AM: Check Emails

Checking my emails was always a top priority, as it helped me stay on top of communications from suppliers, customers, and potential collaborators. This was a crucial part of running a startup, and early responses often meant securing deals or building relationships.

8:00 AM: Get Ready and Breakfast

A quick, efficient routine to fuel me for the day ahead. I didn't waste time here—it was all about getting in gear and staying on track.

9:00 AM – 11:00 AM: Packing Orders & Cold Outreach

This was one of the most critical time blocks of the day. I used these two hours to pack orders, generate shipping labels, and engage with customers. I also did cold outreach, reaching out to potential clients, influencers, or collaborators. I had to skip a few college classes during this time, but this wasn't just business; it was the foundation of my future. Sometimes, I had to choose between education and moving the needle for the business—and most times, the business came first.

12:00 PM: College Classes

While I did attend college, it was often a struggle to balance both worlds. I attended lectures and participated as much as I could, but I also used this time to do backend research, work on tech development, or plan my next moves for the startup. I became an expert at multitasking—sitting at the back of the class, taking notes while also planning my next moves. Sometimes, I would be asked to leave class for working on my startup, but it was just part of the hustle.

1:00 PM – 5:00 PM: College Work and Startup Research

This was my block for focused work, whether it was for college or the business. I would use the time during classes to get research done on competitors, analyze trends, or brainstorm ideas for my startup. There were days when I had to balance college tests with business meetings— honestly, it wasn't ideal, but it was necessary.

6:00 PM – 11:00 PM: Content Creation, Community Engagement, & Team Building

In the evenings, I dedicated my time to content creation. This included writing blog posts, creating social media content, engaging with followers, or doing market research. I also spent time building a team, working with the early members who were helping to get the company off the ground. I focused on growing our community and building relationships that would lead to growth. This was also when I did competitive analysis, keeping an eye on how competitors were performing and what I could do to outperform them.

The Reality of Early Startup Life

Let me tell you—it was hard. I had no time for socializing, no time to eat proper meals, no time to relax. There were no "breaks" in my schedule, and most days, it was just go, go, go. There were times I felt isolated—working on my business with little support, facing the constant pressure to deliver, and dealing with the unpredictable nature of the early startup world.

But looking back, it was all worth it. After about six months of intense work, I had my first real break when my co-founder convinced me to watch a movie. It was a rare moment of respite, and though it felt strange to take a step back, it reminded me of why I was doing all of this—to eventually build a life where I could have a balance between work and life.

Time Management: Not Just About Balance

I won't sugarcoat this for you—when you're in the early stages of your startup, work-life balance simply isn't a reality. It might sound harsh, but you have to understand that balancing work, life, and everything else in between is something you will achieve **only** after you've put in the work. The first few years will be intense. You'll have to sacrifice your social life, your sleep, and, at times, your health to build a business that gives you the life you want in the future.

The Essential Truth: Work Hard, Then You'll Have Balance

It's simple: if you want balance now, go find a job. Jobs come with structure and predictability—they can give you time off, weekends, and holidays. But if you're building something of your own, especially a startup, balance comes **later**. It's something you earn by putting in the work now.

In the early stages, your focus should be entirely on creating something that works, that scales, and that allows you to build the life you've dreamed of. You don't need to worry about balance—just focus on getting things done.

How You Can Create Your Time Table

So, how can you create your own time table? Here's how you can get started:

1. **Assess Your Priorities:** What's the most important thing you can do each day to move your startup forward? Prioritize these tasks above everything else.

2. **Don't Be Afraid to Delegate:** You can't do it all. Build a team or outsource where necessary. Don't try to do everything yourself, as it will quickly lead to burnout.

3. **Break Down Big Tasks:** Start by breaking down huge tasks into manageable chunks. This allows you to focus on one thing at a time and avoid feeling overwhelmed.

4. **Stay Flexible:** Life will throw curveballs, especially in the startup world. Keep your schedule flexible enough to accommodate unexpected situations.

5. **Remember the End Goal:** The hard work you're putting in now is what will allow you to reap the rewards later. Keep that vision front and center as you navigate the challenges.

I recommend reading **"Deep Work: Rules for Focused Success in a Distracted World" by Cal Newport.** This book is an excellent resource for any founder who wants to master time management and productivity. Newport dives into the concept of "deep work," which is the ability to focus without distraction on cognitively demanding tasks. For founders, this concept is crucial because deep, uninterrupted work is what enables you to build, innovate, and create a thriving business amidst all the noise and distractions that come with startup life.

Chapter 4: Embracing Failure – Learning From Setbacks and Bouncing Back

If you're reading this, chances are you have a vision for your startup, and that vision is full of potential, excitement, and possibilities. But here's the thing every founder needs to understand early on—**failure will be a part of your journey**. And no matter how prepared you are, or how much ambition you have, there will be setbacks. But the difference between those who succeed and those who don't isn't that they avoid failure—it's how they **respond to failure**.

This chapter isn't about sugarcoating failure. It's not about painting a picture of a perfect world where everything always goes according to plan. No, it's about accepting failure as an inevitable part of growth and entrepreneurship. It's about embracing failure as your teacher, your guide, and your partner on this unpredictable journey.

The Non-Linear Path of Entrepreneurship

Starting a business is **never** a linear process. It's more like a rollercoaster with steep climbs, sudden drops, unexpected twists, and at times, feeling like you're completely stuck at the bottom. You might wake up one day, feeling on top of the world because you closed a deal, launched a product, or reached a milestone. But the next day, something could go wrong. A product might fail to launch as planned, an investor might pull out, or a marketing campaign might flop.

The key here is to **expect failure**. The greatest entrepreneurs of all time have faced failure. **Failure is not something to avoid—** it's something to learn from, and it's something that you must come to terms with if you're serious about building something meaningful.

Why Failure Is Your Teacher

When you fail, your initial instinct might be to feel defeated, disappointed, or discouraged. These feelings are completely normal. However, if you can shift your mindset around failure and see it as **data**—as feedback on what needs to change—you'll be able to take those painful moments and turn them into powerful learning opportunities.

Think about it this way: failure isn't a destination—it's a **learning checkpoint**. Every mistake you make, every time things don't go according to plan, is simply your mind and body telling you, "Here's what you need to adjust to move forward."

Failure allows you to:

- **Test your assumptions**: Did your initial idea really meet the market's needs? Was there something in your product, marketing, or business model that needed adjustment?

- **Adapt and iterate**: Once you understand why something didn't work, you can make changes. The key is to test, fail, iterate, and improve.

- **Strengthen resilience**: Overcoming failure isn't just about fixing a mistake. It's about building the emotional stamina to withstand the next failure and learn even faster.

- **Develop critical thinking**: Failure forces you to **think deeply**. You'll reflect on your processes, your decisions, and your actions. It sharpens your judgment, intuition, and strategic thinking.

Failing Forward

One of the most powerful concepts in entrepreneurship is the idea of **"failing forward."** This means that each time you fail, you don't just stumble backward. You take that failure, analyze it, and use it as fuel to move forward—stronger, smarter, and better prepared for the next challenge.

A failure that doesn't lead to growth is a wasted failure. But if you can **reflect on what went wrong**, make the necessary changes, and keep moving forward with a newfound clarity, that failure becomes a step toward your ultimate success.

The Importance of Resilience

The ability to bounce back from failure is what separates successful entrepreneurs from those who give up. **Resilience** is what allows you to keep going when everything feels like it's falling apart. It's about not letting setbacks derail your vision.

Here's a simple but powerful framework to develop resilience in your entrepreneurial journey:

1. **Acknowledge the disappointment**: It's okay to feel frustrated or upset when something doesn't work. Recognizing your emotions is part of the process.

2. **Understand what went wrong**: Sit down and analyze what happened. Look for patterns, and ask yourself, "What could I have done differently?"

3. **Adapt your strategy**: Once you understand what went wrong, take proactive steps to adjust. Make a plan to move forward.

4. **Keep your vision in sight**: The bigger picture is your vision. Your failure might be a temporary setback, but your vision should always be your guiding star.

5. **Celebrate small wins**: After a failure, it's easy to lose sight of your progress. Celebrate the small

successes and build on them as you continue to evolve.

Real-Life Example: How Failure Led to Success

Think of famous entrepreneurs who turned failure into success. Take **Thomas Edison**, for instance. He failed thousands of times before inventing the light bulb. Or **Steve Jobs**, who was fired from his own company, only to return years later and turn Apple into one of the most valuable companies in the world. These entrepreneurs didn't see failure as a roadblock—they saw it as an opportunity to refine their approach, improve their products, and become stronger leaders.

As a founder, you'll face difficult moments—there's no way around it. But these moments are what make the difference between building a business that fails and building one that lasts. **Failure is where the magic happens.**

Key Takeaways

- Failure is inevitable—embrace it as a part of your entrepreneurial journey.

- **Failure is not the opposite of success**—it's a stepping stone on the path to success.
- Learn from each setback, analyze what went wrong, and use it to improve and iterate.
- Build resilience by focusing on your vision and adapting your approach when things don't go as planned.

Book Recommendation

To dive deeper into the concept of learning from failure and building resilience, I highly recommend **"The Lean Startup" by Eric Ries.** This book provides a methodology for developing businesses in a systematic and structured way, using feedback loops, experiments, and learning from failure to create scalable companies. It's a must-read for any founder navigating the rough terrain of the early stages of a startup.

Chapter 5: Turning Ideas into Action – Moving from Dreamer to Doer

As an aspiring founder, you're likely bursting with ideas. You have a vision of your dream business, and the possibilities seem endless. But here's the truth: **dreaming about your business is easy.** The real challenge lies in transforming those dreams into tangible actions that move the needle toward success.

In this chapter, we'll take a hard look at what it means to transition from being a "dreamer" to a "doer" in your entrepreneurial journey. We'll talk about how to move beyond the abstract concept of your business and start taking deliberate, actionable steps. Because, in the end, it's not the ideas that make or break a business—it's the execution.

The Struggle of Turning Ideas Into Action

There's a reason most people are stuck in the "dreamer" phase. **Ideas are easy**—they come to us at all hours of the day and night. They're exciting, creative, and full of potential. But, here's the catch: **ideas alone**

won't create a business. Without action, those dreams remain exactly that—dreams.

Taking action can feel overwhelming. You might have a big vision, but starting feels like a daunting task. The path from having an idea to actually executing it can seem like a chasm, and that can lead to **analysis paralysis**—a state where you're constantly planning, perfecting, and thinking about what to do, but never actually doing it.

The real challenge is bridging that gap. **It's about taking that first step, even when you don't have all the answers.** It's about starting somewhere, anywhere, and building momentum along the way.

Overcoming the Fear of Starting

One of the biggest roadblocks to action is fear. Fear of failure, fear of rejection, fear of not knowing enough—it's all paralyzing. When you don't know exactly what you're doing, it's easy to hold yourself back and tell yourself you're not ready.

But here's a little secret: **you'll never be fully "ready."** The conditions will never be perfect, and there will always be unknowns. The most successful founders are those who've learned to embrace uncertainty and take the first step anyway.

Start by **accepting that it's okay to be imperfect.** You don't need to have every detail figured out. What matters most is **getting started**. You can refine and improve as you go along, but the most important thing is to take that first action—no matter how small it is.

Building Momentum Through Small Wins

The key to turning ideas into action is to **break your big goals down into smaller, manageable tasks.** Instead of focusing on the huge, overwhelming task of "launching a business," break it down into smaller chunks: research your target market, validate your idea, create a business plan, find a supplier, and so on.

Each of these smaller tasks can be completed in a day or a week, and as you cross them off your list, you'll feel momentum building. The psychological impact of small wins is huge. **Every time you**

complete a task, you build confidence in your ability to follow through. This confidence will fuel your desire to keep going and take more action.

The Power of Setting Clear, Actionable Goals

If you don't have a clear vision for what you need to accomplish, it's easy to feel scattered and directionless. To avoid this, set **specific, actionable goals** that move you closer to turning your idea into a reality.

Here's how to structure your goals:

- **Make them specific**: Instead of vague goals like "grow my business," make them concrete: "reach out to 10 potential customers this week."

- **Set deadlines**: Deadlines create urgency and help you stay focused. Without them, it's easy to procrastinate.

- **Track your progress**: Use tools like project management apps (e.g., Trello, Asana, Notion) to break down your larger goals into smaller tasks and track your progress.

A great way to structure these goals is by using the **SMART framework**: Specific, Measurable, Achievable, Relevant, and Time-bound. This will keep your actions grounded in reality and ensure that each step you take gets you closer to your vision.

The Importance of Execution Over Perfection

Another barrier to turning ideas into action is the pursuit of perfection. Many founders get stuck in the endless cycle of refining their idea or product until it's "perfect" before they ever launch it. But here's the truth: **perfection is the enemy of progress.**

When you're in the early stages of your startup, focus on execution, not perfection. You need to get something out into the world to test and iterate. Don't wait for everything to be flawless before you start. Launch your idea as a **minimum viable product (MVP)**—this is the simplest version of your product that solves the core problem for your target audience. You can always improve and build upon it as you get feedback from real users.

The key takeaway here is: Start messy, and get better as you go. Perfect doesn't exist in the early stages, and trying to make everything perfect will only delay your progress.

Turning Ideas Into Action Every Day

In the early stages of your startup, your days will be full. Between building the product, validating it, talking to customers, and handling the countless administrative tasks that come with running a business, time will always be tight. But turning your ideas into action doesn't have to be overwhelming. **The secret is consistency.**

Here's how to consistently turn your ideas into action:

1. **Schedule time to work on your business every day.** Even if it's just 30 minutes, set aside dedicated time to work on your startup each day.

2. **Break down your big ideas into daily tasks.** Instead of tackling

everything at once, focus on one thing at a time.

3. **Track your progress.** Keep a journal or use an app to track your wins and challenges. This will help you stay motivated and on track.

Consistency, no matter how small, will compound over time and bring you closer to your goals. The more action you take, the clearer your path will become.

From Dreamer to Doer: A Mental Shift

Finally, it's important to make a mental shift. Being a "doer" isn't about having all the answers, it's about **taking action in the face of uncertainty**. The best entrepreneurs don't wait until they have everything figured out—they take the leap and learn as they go.

If you want to move from dreamer to doer, ask yourself: "What's the smallest, most actionable thing I can do today to move my startup forward?" Even if it's something tiny, take that first step. The next day, take another. And soon, you'll find that your ideas aren't just dreams anymore—they're becoming your reality.

Book Recommendation

To help guide you through the process of turning your ideas into action, I highly recommend **"The War of Art" by Steven Pressfield**. This book dives into the inner battle that every creative person faces when it comes to overcoming resistance and taking action. It's a short read, but packed with powerful insights on how to break through procrastination and get started—now.

Chapter 6: Building Your MVP – From Idea to First Product

When you're in the early stages of starting your business, one of the most important—and often the most difficult—steps is building your **Minimum Viable Product (MVP)**. An MVP is the first tangible version of your product, built with the simplest features that solve the core problem for your customers. It's not about perfection; it's about **getting your idea into the hands of real users** as quickly as possible.

This chapter is designed to push you to stop overthinking, stop planning endlessly, and start building your MVP. It's all about turning your idea into a real, functional product, even if it's a rough version of what you ultimately want to create.

What is an MVP?

Before we dive into the process, let's break down what an MVP is.

A **Minimum Viable Product** is the simplest version of your product that still delivers value to your customers. It has just enough features to be functional and meet the needs of your early adopters, who are the first group of users willing to try your product. An MVP is not a finished, polished product. It's a starting point—something that allows you to test your idea, gather feedback, and learn what works and what doesn't before you invest more time and resources into building the final version.

Think of your MVP as a **prototype**. It should answer one question: **Does this product solve the problem I'm trying to address?**

The Importance of MVP in Your Startup Journey

The importance of an MVP lies in its ability to help you **validate your idea quickly**. In the early stages of a startup, **time and money are precious**. Instead of pouring months (or years) into building a fully fleshed-out product, your MVP lets you gather feedback, test the market, and figure out if there's actual demand for your idea.

It's also your best defense against **perfectionism**. Many aspiring founders get stuck in the endless loop of tweaking their idea or designing the "perfect" product before even testing it. The truth is, you **don't know what's perfect** until you test it with real customers. An MVP lets you test your assumptions, pivot when needed, and get to market faster.

Step 1: Define the Core Problem You're Solving

Before you can build your MVP, you need to be crystal clear on the **problem you're solving**. This is the foundation of your product. If you can't articulate the problem in a sentence or two, chances are your product isn't well-defined yet.

Ask yourself:

- **What is the problem I'm solving?**
- **Who is experiencing this problem?**
- **Why is my solution better than what's already out there?**

These questions should be your guiding light as you build your MVP. A good MVP addresses a clear pain point that's important to your target audience. Without a solid understanding of the problem, you're just guessing at what features to include, and that's a recipe for failure.

Step 2: Identify the Most Essential Features

Now that you've defined the problem, it's time to figure out **what features your MVP absolutely needs** to solve that problem. Remember, this isn't about building the ultimate product with all the bells and whistles. Your MVP should only include the features that **solve the core problem** and allow you to gather data on its effectiveness.

To identify the essential features, ask yourself:

- **What's the smallest version of this product that will solve the problem?**
- **Which features will directly solve the pain points of your users?**
- **What can be left out for now?**

When building your MVP, think of it as the **bare minimum** that still provides value.

Everything else is **nice-to-have**, and it can come later.

Step 3: Build, Don't Plan Forever

One of the biggest mistakes founders make is planning endlessly. You may feel like you need to perfect your product before you build it, but this is a dangerous trap. **Planning is important, but action is essential.** You will learn much more by actually building and testing than by endlessly discussing what your product will be like.

Here's the secret: **Start small.** You don't need to build the full product. You just need to create the simplest version of your idea that solves the problem. Don't overcomplicate things. If your idea involves an app, your MVP might just be a basic prototype with the core feature working. If it's a physical product, start with a mock-up or a basic version that works.

At this stage, focus on **getting something functional out the door**. It doesn't need to be pretty, it doesn't need to be perfect—it just needs to work.

Step 4: Test with Real Customers

Once you have your MVP, it's time to **get it in front of real users**. This is where the magic happens. You'll start to get feedback on what works, what doesn't, and what needs to be improved.

Don't wait for perfect feedback. Early users may not give you the most polished responses, but they'll help you **identify the key issues** with your product. Focus on the big picture: Do they understand the value of your product? Does it solve the problem they care about? Are they willing to pay for it?

The best way to get feedback is to **interview your users**. Ask open-ended questions about their experience with your MVP. Be humble and ready to listen to critical feedback—it's the only way to improve.

Step 5: Iterate Based on Feedback

Your MVP is not a final product. It's a **starting point**, and you'll need to make improvements based on the feedback you get from your users.

Here's where the power of iteration comes in. Once you've gathered feedback, take the time to make changes and improve your product. If users don't understand a certain feature, fix it. If they think something's missing, add it in. Your MVP will evolve over time as you learn more about your customers and what they need.

Iterating quickly is a core skill in the startup world. The faster you learn from your users, the faster you can adapt and build a product that truly meets their needs.

Step 6: Launch and Keep It Simple

You've now created an MVP, tested it with users, and iterated on it. It's time to launch—no more waiting, no more perfectionism. It's time to get your product into the market and **start building your brand**.

Keep your launch simple. Don't worry about fancy marketing campaigns or spending a lot of money. Start by reaching out to your early adopters—those people who will be excited to use your product. Engage with your customers and continue to listen to their feedback as you improve the product.

Step 7: Continue the Learning Loop

Building an MVP is just the beginning. The key is to keep learning, iterating, and improving. Every time you launch a new version, test it with users again. Get their feedback, make adjustments, and launch again. This feedback loop is what will drive your startup forward and eventually help you build a product that customers love.

Book Recommendation

To support your MVP journey, I recommend reading **"Zero to One" by Peter Thiel**. This book is all about building something unique, and Thiel emphasizes the importance of starting with a simple but powerful vision. It guides you on how to think about innovation, the future of startups, and how to approach creating a product that stands out from the competition. It's an essential read for founders who want to create a product with true market value and not just follow trends.

Chapter 7: Finding Product-Market Fit – The Key to Sustainable Growth

You've done the hard work. You've crafted your product, refined your MVP, and gathered initial feedback from users. Now, the ultimate test begins: **finding product-market fit**. This is the stage where your startup either takes off or stagnates. But what exactly is product-market fit? How do you know when you've found it? And how do you get there if you're still searching for it?

What is Product-Market Fit?

Simply put, product-market fit (PMF) occurs when your product meets the needs of a specific target market in a way that drives demand. It's the sweet spot where customers love your product, and it resonates deeply with their needs. At this stage, your product starts to sell itself, and growth is organic.

You may have heard that achieving product-market fit is a milestone that every successful startup strives for. But let me be clear—it's not a one-time event. It's a process, and sometimes, it's a long journey of trial, error, and adaptation. **There's no shortcut.** However, once you find it, you're in a great position for sustainable growth.

How to Know You've Hit Product-Market Fit

Many founders get stuck trying to define what PMF looks like for their business. Here's the reality: there's no universal marker that says, "Congratulations, you've made it!" But here are some signs that indicate you might be on the right track:

1. **Customer Demand Is Growing**: This is perhaps the most visible sign. If you have a steady increase in customer inquiries, your product is being recommended by word-of-mouth, and your acquisition channels are becoming more effective, you're likely in the right direction.

2. **High Retention Rates**: If users who try your product continue to use it, that's a big win. High retention rates signal that customers are finding value in what you're offering. After all,

customers who don't see value will simply churn.

3. **Customers Are Willing to Pay for It**: Your product needs to move beyond being just something people try—it needs to be something they are willing to pay for. When you start seeing people pull out their wallets consistently, you're likely hitting PMF.

4. **Customer Feedback**: When customers are not only giving positive feedback but are also sharing how your product is improving their lives, you've got something meaningful on your hands. The passion and loyalty of your customer base are the best signals that you're on track.

5. **Sales Are Growing Faster Than You Can Keep Up**: Growth that feels out of control can be overwhelming, but it's also a key sign of PMF. When demand outpaces supply, it's an exciting moment—you've found a product that people want, and now

you need to scale up to meet that demand.

If You Haven't Found Product-Market Fit Yet...

Don't panic. Finding PMF can take time, and every startup will go through different phases before they get there. **The key is persistence and iteration.** If your product hasn't yet found its sweet spot in the market, it's essential to:

1. **Gather Feedback Relentlessly**: Keep talking to your customers, both happy and unhappy ones. Understand their pain points, why they are choosing your product, and where you can improve. This feedback loop will help you fine-tune your offering.

2. **Focus on a Niche**: At first, you might be tempted to cater to as many people as possible. However, finding a niche market where you can solve a specific problem more effectively is often the best route to PMF. Once

you dominate a small segment, you can expand.

3. **Don't Be Afraid to Pivot**: If your initial idea isn't getting traction, it might be time to change direction. This doesn't mean abandoning everything, but it could mean tweaking the product, the features, or even the target audience. A successful pivot could be the key to unlocking PMF.

4. **Measure and Iterate**: As much as you want to move forward, the reality is that you need to keep testing your assumptions. Continually measuring your product's usage, understanding user behaviors, and adapting to their needs is essential. Data will show you the way.

5. **Be Ready to Adapt to Market Changes**: Product-market fit doesn't happen in a vacuum. External factors like competition, market trends, or shifts in customer expectations can all influence your journey. Be

prepared to adjust and adapt as the landscape changes.

Why Product-Market Fit Matters

Once you've found product-market fit, your startup enters a new phase—growth. This is where everything changes. You'll see a rapid increase in demand, which opens up opportunities for scaling, expanding into new markets, and even diversifying your product line. Without PMF, your startup is like a ship adrift at sea—it's hard to navigate, and growth is unpredictable.

However, achieving product-market fit isn't a one-and-done deal. **Your product will need to evolve as market needs change.** Achieving PMF is just the beginning of a continuous process of improvement, but once you have it, you're in a position to focus on scaling up, acquiring more customers, and delivering consistent value.

Moving from Finding Product-Market Fit to Scaling

Once you've established that you've found product-market fit, your next challenge is scaling your startup. You've validated your product, and the market is responding positively. Now, it's time to take that success and grow it into a thriving business. But scaling brings its own set of challenges, from hiring the right team to managing operations, funding, and increasing marketing efforts.

Finding product-market fit is often seen as the foundation for sustainable growth. With it, you can start investing more heavily in your marketing strategy, refining your product, and building the operational infrastructure to meet the growing demand.

Key Takeaways:

- Product-market fit is the critical phase when your product meets the needs of the market, driving demand and ensuring sustainability.

- Look for signs like high customer retention, demand growth, and users who are willing to pay for your product.

- If you haven't found PMF yet, don't worry. Gather customer feedback, focus on a niche, and be willing to pivot if necessary.

- Achieving PMF sets the stage for scaling, but it requires continuous iteration and adaptation.

Finding product-market fit is a dynamic, iterative process. It takes time, feedback, and persistence. But once you achieve it, you're on the path to building a sustainable, growth-oriented startup.

Book Recommendation

For a more targeted and insightful approach to finding product-market fit, I recommend **"Play Bigger: How Pirates, Dreamers, and Innovators Create the Markets They Own" by Al Ramadan, Dave Peterson, Christopher Lochhead, and Kevin Maney**.

This book goes beyond the basics of product-market fit and delves into the concept of **category creation**, which is a critical component for scaling and establishing dominance in your market. The authors highlight how the most successful startups and businesses don't just find product-market fit—they create entire markets around their products.

Chapter 8: Sales and Customer Acquisition – Turning Leads Into Loyal Customers

Sales, especially in the early days of a startup, can often feel like an uphill battle. You're starting with nothing—no reputation, no customer base, and probably not much budget for marketing. Yet, without customers, there's no business. The truth is, sales are the lifeblood of any startup, and how you approach customer acquisition can make or break your company. This chapter is designed to help you move away from the traditional "hard sell" mentality and focus on building relationships that convert to loyal customers.

Redefining Sales: From Push to Pull

Sales in today's world are no longer about pushing a product onto unwilling buyers. In fact, the idea of "hard selling" has become almost obsolete. Instead, modern sales revolve around attracting the right customers who already want what you offer. You're not forcing a solution on someone; you're helping them realize that your solution is the right fit for their needs.

To succeed, it's critical to think of sales not as a transactional exchange, but as the beginning of a long-term relationship. When you approach sales with a mindset of providing value, you'll not only increase your conversion rates, but you'll also cultivate a loyal customer base that will return to you time and time again.

Start with Understanding Your Customers

Before you can begin selling, you must first understand who your customers are. It may seem obvious, but many founders skip this crucial step. You need to know everything about your target audience: their pain points, their desires, their motivations, and their struggles. Without this deep understanding, any marketing or sales pitch will miss the mark.

The more granular you get with your customer research, the better you can tailor your messaging to resonate with them. Are you solving a specific problem for your customers? How does your product or service make their lives easier, better, or more enjoyable? Once you have a clear picture of your ideal customer, you can craft your pitch accordingly.

Crafting the Right Message

Your messaging is the bridge between your startup and your customers. It has to speak directly to their needs and desires. Don't just focus on features—focus on **benefits**. Instead of telling people what your product does, show them how it will improve their lives.

For example, if you sell a project management tool, don't just list the features. Instead, explain how it will help a busy professional save hours each week, reduce stress, and stay organized. Speak to the emotional benefits as well as the practical ones.

When crafting your message, focus on **clarity**. Avoid jargon, buzzwords, and anything that could confuse your audience. You're not trying to impress them with your knowledge of industry terms; you're trying to communicate why your solution is the one they've been looking for.

Building Trust and Social Proof

At the start of your journey, you may not have a strong reputation. In fact, you may have no reputation at all. This is why **trust** is so important in the sales process. People won't buy from you if they don't trust you, especially in the early stages when your startup is still new and untested.

Building trust doesn't have to be complicated. Start by being **transparent** about your process, your pricing, and your values. Share customer testimonials, case studies, and social proof whenever possible. If your product or service has helped others, make sure potential customers know about it.

Remember that trust is earned, not given, so focus on delivering an exceptional customer experience at every step. From the first interaction with your brand to the post-purchase follow-up, ensure that customers feel valued and respected.

Nurturing Leads: The Power of Follow-Up

Acquiring a lead is just the first step in the sales process. The real work begins when you start nurturing those leads. **Follow-up** is often the most overlooked and undervalued part of the sales journey, but it's crucial to turning leads into loyal customers.

Not everyone is going to buy immediately. Some leads need time to think, others need more information, and some might just need a gentle reminder that your product is still available. Instead of waiting for leads to come to you, actively engage with them. Send personalized follow-up emails, offer additional content that can help them make a decision, and make it easy for them to reach out to you.

The goal is to stay top-of-mind without being pushy. Make your communication **relevant**, **helpful**, and **non-salesy**. Over time, this will build a rapport and trust with your potential customers, ultimately making it easier to convert them into buyers.

Turning a Sale Into a Relationship

A sale should never be the end of the conversation; it should be the beginning of a relationship. The most successful startups focus not just on customer acquisition, but on **customer retention**. Building long-term relationships with your customers ensures that they will return, recommend your product to others, and become advocates for your brand.

Your post-purchase process is just as important as your pre-purchase efforts. Make sure you're following up with customers after they've bought your product, asking for feedback, and offering assistance if needed. Providing outstanding customer service and showing genuine interest in their satisfaction will go a long way in securing customer loyalty.

A customer who has had a positive experience with your company is more likely to come back—and more likely to recommend you to others. Word of mouth is a powerful tool in customer acquisition, and it's often the best form of marketing you can get.

Your Sales Strategy: A Plan for Success

Creating a successful sales strategy doesn't happen overnight. It requires careful planning, execution, and continuous iteration. Start by identifying your customer personas, crafting your messaging, and setting goals for your sales pipeline. From there, you can begin to experiment with different outreach methods—whether it's cold emailing, social selling, or content marketing—and see what resonates with your target audience.

As you begin generating leads, track your progress and refine your strategy based on the results. Sales are rarely a one-size-fits-all approach, so be prepared to tweak your tactics as you learn more about what works and what doesn't.

Above all, remember that sales are about **relationships**, not transactions. When you prioritize building trust and offering value to your customers, sales will naturally follow.

Book Recommendation:

To deepen your understanding of customer acquisition and sales in the modern world, I highly recommend **"The Challenger Sale: Taking Control of the Customer Conversation" by Matthew Dixon and Brent Adamson.** This book offers a fresh perspective on selling, focusing on teaching salespeople how to challenge their customers' thinking and guide them toward the right solution. It's an essential read for any founder who wants to refine their sales strategy and turn leads into loyal, long-term customers.

Chapter 9: Bootstrapping vs. Fundraising – The Right Approach for Your Startup

As a startup founder, one of the most crucial decisions you'll face early on is how to finance your venture. Do you bootstrap the business—funding it yourself—or do you seek external investment? The answer isn't always clear-cut, and it depends on your unique circumstances, goals, and the type of business you're building.

This chapter explores both options in-depth, offering you a comprehensive understanding of **bootstrapping** and **fundraising**, including the advantages, disadvantages, and when one might be a better fit over the other. The decision is personal, and there's no "one-size-fits-all" approach. What matters is understanding both paths and aligning them with your vision and strategy.

Bootstrapping – The Power of Self-Reliance

Bootstrapping is the art of building your startup without relying on external funding. It means you're funding the company out of your own pocket, using personal savings, revenue from customers, or reinvesting profits back into the business. Bootstrapping is often seen as the more difficult option, but it's also the path that offers the most control, flexibility, and freedom.

Advantages of Bootstrapping

1. **Full Control Over Your Business:** When you bootstrap, you don't have investors or venture capitalists telling you what to do. You have complete control over your company's direction, decisions, and strategies. You get to determine your roadmap without worrying about meeting external expectations or giving up equity in your company.

2. **Less Pressure to Scale Quickly:** Bootstrapping often means slow and steady growth. This can be beneficial for founders who prefer a more organic pace, where they can experiment, learn, and scale on their own terms. There's no need to rush to meet unrealistic targets, which is

often the case with investor-driven companies.

3. **No Equity Dilution:** Since you're not taking outside money, you don't have to give away any equity. In the early stages, retaining 100% ownership of your company can be a powerful motivator and allow you to keep the business aligned with your values and goals.

4. **Financial Discipline:** Bootstrapping forces you to be frugal and disciplined with your spending. Every dollar counts, and you learn how to make the most out of limited resources. This can cultivate a strong mindset for managing money and building a sustainable business.

Challenges of Bootstrapping

1. **Limited Resources:** The biggest challenge of bootstrapping is the lack of external funding. Without outside investment, your growth is limited to your own resources. This can mean slower scaling, fewer hires, and

potentially less marketing reach. You need to be creative and resourceful to make things work.

2. **Higher Personal Risk:** When you bootstrap, you're essentially betting on yourself and your idea. It's your personal savings, time, and effort that are at risk, which can put a lot of pressure on you. If your startup doesn't work out, it could be a major financial setback for you personally.

3. **Slower Growth:** Bootstrapped companies often grow more slowly than funded ones. Without external capital, you may have to take on additional work yourself or rely on slower marketing tactics and product development. Rapid growth may be harder to achieve, especially in competitive industries.

4. **Limited Networking:** Without investors, you may miss out on the valuable network that comes with fundraising. Many investors bring more than just money—they offer

mentorship, industry connections, and advice. Without this network, you'll need to find other ways to build relationships and gain guidance.

Fundraising – Accessing the Power of External Capital

Fundraising, on the other hand, is the process of raising capital from external sources like venture capitalists (VCs), angel investors, crowdfunding, or through other means of public or private funding. This path allows you to access large sums of money that can be used for rapid scaling, product development, or aggressive marketing campaigns. While fundraising can offer a quick infusion of cash, it also comes with its own set of challenges.

Advantages of Fundraising

1. **Access to Significant Capital:** Fundraising allows you to scale your business quickly. With access to capital, you can invest in hiring a team, developing your product, marketing, and scaling operations at a pace that would be impossible to

achieve with personal savings alone. This is critical if you are in a competitive market that requires heavy investment upfront.

2. **Mentorship and Guidance:** Many investors bring more to the table than just money. They offer invaluable industry expertise, strategic advice, and mentoring that can help you navigate complex business challenges. They often act as partners in your journey, helping you avoid common mistakes and connect with the right people.

3. **Faster Growth and Market Penetration:** With external funding, you can take calculated risks and push your startup to grow faster. This can help you build a stronger brand presence, gain market share quickly, and compete effectively with other players in your industry. Fundraising accelerates everything—product development, team building, and customer acquisition.

4. **Credibility and Networking:** Securing investment from reputable investors can lend credibility to your startup. It can help you attract customers, partners, and top-tier talent who may be hesitant to work with an unproven business. Additionally, investors often have extensive networks that you can tap into for opportunities.

Challenges of Fundraising

1. **Loss of Control and Equity:** One of the biggest downsides to fundraising is the dilution of your ownership in the business. Investors often want a say in the direction of the company, and they may require equity or decision-making power in exchange for their investment. This can lead to disagreements over how the company should grow, as you may have to compromise on your vision.

2. **Pressure to Scale Rapidly:** Investors expect returns, and they expect them quickly. When you raise money,

there's often significant pressure to scale fast, hit revenue targets, and grow at a pace that may not always align with your long-term vision. This fast-paced growth can cause a startup to lose its footing or veer off track.

3. **Time-Consuming and Complex Process:** Fundraising is time-consuming and requires significant effort. Pitching to investors, negotiating terms, and preparing for due diligence takes time away from running your business. You also have to ensure that your startup is structured in a way that is appealing to investors, which may require significant changes.

4. **Potential for Misaligned Expectations:** Investors have different motivations than founders. While you're focused on building a sustainable, mission-driven business, investors may be more focused on quick returns. Misaligned expectations can lead to tension, and

in some cases, disagreements that impact the company's growth and direction.

Which Path Is Right for You?

Choosing between bootstrapping and fundraising is a personal decision, and there's no right or wrong answer. It depends on your goals, your tolerance for risk, and the type of business you want to build.

- **If you're focused on building a business at your own pace, maintaining full control, and are okay with slower growth, bootstrapping may be the right choice for you.**

- **If you're looking for rapid growth, larger market opportunities, and the support of experienced investors, fundraising may be the right route.**

There's also a hybrid approach—starting out by bootstrapping until you hit a certain milestone, and then seeking investment once you have proof of concept or some traction.

Real-Life Examples:

- **Bootstrap Example:** Basecamp (formerly Zerodha) is a well-known example of a company that bootstrapped to success. Despite having the opportunity to raise funds, the founders chose to remain independent, keeping full control over the company. They built their product at their own pace and grew steadily without external interference.

- **Fundraising Example:** A prime example of a startup that successfully raised funds is Airbnb. The company initially struggled but was able to secure investment from venture capitalists that allowed them to grow rapidly, reach a global market, and revolutionize the hospitality industry.

Final Thoughts

Your decision between bootstrapping and fundraising will depend on your startup's needs and your personal preferences. Whether you bootstrap or fundraise, the key to success lies in your ability to execute on your vision and build a business that provides value to your customers. Stay true to your goals, and remember that both paths—though different—lead to the same destination: building a successful, sustainable business.

Book Recommendation
"Traction: Get a Grip on Your Business" by Gino Wickman
For founders focused on bootstrapping, **"Traction"** is a must-read. This book offers practical and actionable advice on how to gain control of your business and achieve sustainable growth without relying on external funding. Gino Wickman introduces the Entrepreneurial Operating System (EOS), a framework that helps entrepreneurs simplify their businesses, set clear goals, and track progress effectively. The book covers how to manage your resources

efficiently, build a strong team, and implement processes that allow you to scale your startup while staying true to your bootstrapped roots. If you're serious about building traction with limited resources, this book is an invaluable guide.

Chapter 10: Building a Lean Team – Hiring Your First Employees or Contractors

Building a startup is like building a house—you need the right foundation and a few key players to get started. The journey of hiring your first team members is one of the most pivotal moments in any founder's path. It's not about hiring a huge team, it's about building a lean, efficient, and agile team that aligns with your vision, values, and goals.

The Lean Team Mindset

When you're starting out, every decision you make should have the goal of maximizing efficiency. You don't need a massive team to build a successful startup, especially in the early stages. In fact, most successful startups start with just a handful of core people who are committed, versatile, and willing to roll up their sleeves. A lean team isn't just about cutting costs—it's about being strategic and resourceful, keeping things simple and focused.

It's easy to get caught up in the idea that you need a full-fledged team of employees to get things off the ground, but that's a common pitfall. Your early hires should bring in complementary skills that fill the gaps you have as the founder. They should share your passion and vision, but also offer expertise that you might not have.

Defining Roles: Quality Over Quantity

Instead of trying to hire a team for every function, prioritize a few core roles. Focus on hiring people who can wear multiple hats and handle a variety of tasks. The key is hiring for versatility, commitment, and a shared sense of purpose. These first hires will be the people who are with you when you're in the trenches, working late nights, and celebrating early wins. They must be people who understand the unpredictable nature of startups and are eager to face those challenges head-on.

Here's a blueprint for your first hires:

1. **Co-founder/Partner (If you haven't already):**
   Your first hire might actually be a co-founder. If you're not already working with one, consider finding someone whose skills complement yours. This

person can be a technical co-founder if you're more on the business side, or a business co-founder if you're the product or technical lead. A strong partnership is critical to balancing the workload and tackling the challenges that will inevitably arise.

2. **Marketing Specialist or Growth Hacker:**
   In the early stages, marketing is everything. While you might be doing marketing yourself in the beginning, eventually you'll need someone to help you scale your marketing efforts, even if it's just part-time or on a contractual basis. Look for someone who is familiar with guerrilla marketing tactics, content creation, and growth hacking strategies that can bring quick results with minimal budget.

3. **Customer Support:**
   Your customers are your first product testers, and their feedback will shape your product. A customer support representative (or contractor) can

help you stay connected to your customers, solve issues, and gather insights to improve your offerings. A strong customer support experience can set your brand apart in the early stages, building loyalty and trust among the first adopters of your product.

4. **Operations/Project Manager:** Operations are the backbone of your startup, and in the early days, you'll need someone who can take charge of day-to-day tasks, manage deadlines, and make sure things are running smoothly. A good operations manager will allow you to focus on scaling the business while they handle the internal workings of your startup, making sure you're meeting goals and staying on track.

5. **Freelancers and Contractors:** You don't need to hire full-time employees for everything. In the early stages, freelancers or contractors can be an excellent solution for things like graphic design,

copywriting, or web development. Hiring contractors allows you to scale your team as needed without committing to full-time salaries. This gives you the flexibility to adjust your workforce depending on your business needs and budget.

Hiring Smart: The Right Fit, Not the Right Resume

While you're looking for the best skills, don't overlook the importance of culture fit. You need to hire people who share your values, understand your startup's mission, and have a growth mindset. In the early days, technical skills can always be taught, but a strong cultural fit and the ability to work in an agile, high-pressure environment are non-negotiable.

Here are a few things to look for in potential hires:

- **Versatility:** Look for individuals who can adapt to shifting roles, especially when the startup landscape changes quickly.

- **Passion:** Your first employees should believe in your vision and understand the mission you're working towards.

- **Resourcefulness:** In the startup world, problems are unpredictable, so you need team members who are good problem solvers and can think on their feet.

- **Communication Skills:** Clear communication is vital in a small team where everyone wears multiple hats.

Managing Your Lean Team

Once you've hired your initial team, it's crucial to manage them effectively. With a lean team, each person is integral to your startup's success. You won't have layers of management or a formal structure in place—at least not in the early stages. Instead, focus on open communication, collaboration, and building a strong work culture that promotes mutual respect and accountability.

Use the following strategies to keep your team engaged and motivated:

- **Frequent check-ins:** Keep communication flowing, especially in a lean team. Weekly or bi-weekly check-ins can help align everyone with the business's goals.

- **Transparency:** Keep your team informed about the company's progress, challenges, and any upcoming changes. Transparency builds trust and keeps everyone on the same page.

- **Celebrate wins, big and small:** It's easy to get caught up in the day-to-day grind, but don't forget to celebrate your wins with your team. Whether it's hitting a sales target or launching a new feature, recognition goes a long way in keeping morale high.

Outsourcing: Knowing When to Seek Help

As your business grows, there will be moments when your internal team just doesn't have the capacity to take on more tasks. This is where outsourcing comes in. Whether it's for marketing campaigns, product development, or customer service, knowing when and how to outsource is an important skill for any founder. When outsourcing, always focus on finding the right partners who align with your vision and work ethic.

Outsourcing can be particularly useful in areas where you don't have the expertise. For instance, if you need a professional to handle legal or accounting issues, hiring a legal firm or freelance accountant can free up your time to focus on growing the business. Similarly, when it comes to design or development, using freelancers or agencies can help you scale faster without the overhead costs of full-time employees.

The Bottom Line: Build Slowly and Smartly

Building a lean team is not about rushing to hire the first people you can find. It's about thinking strategically and ensuring that each person you bring on board is an asset that adds value to your company. Your initial hires will set the tone for your company culture and the future of your business. So, take your time, hire the right people, and build a team that can grow with you.

Start with just a few key players who believe in your vision, wear multiple hats, and are committed to the long-term success of the company. By doing so, you'll create a solid foundation for your startup to scale and succeed, even in the most challenging times.

Book Recommendation:

"Recruited: A Guide to Hiring Great People for Your Startup" by Geoff Smart and Randy Street
This book offers deep insights into the hiring process, especially when it comes to startups. It's an excellent resource for founders who are looking to build a lean team that can support their vision and growth. The authors provide a structured approach to finding, interviewing, and hiring people who are a perfect fit for your startup, ensuring you have the best team on board to take your business to the next level.

Chapter 11: Creating Relationships – Networking and Mentorship for Startup Growth

In the world of startups, networking often gets a bad rap. It's too easy to think of networking as a numbers game: attend events, collect business cards, and hope for something good to come from it. But real networking—the kind that truly moves the needle for your business—is about building genuine, lasting relationships, not just transactional connections. This chapter is all about changing the way you think about networking and mentorship, so you can forge relationships that will propel your startup forward.

The Shift: From Transactional to Relational

When you're starting out, you might find yourself in a rush to connect with everyone—investors, potential customers, influencers, advisors, etc. And while these connections might seem important, it's essential to understand that the most valuable relationships are those that grow organically, over time, and are based on trust and mutual benefit.

Real networking isn't about sending out a LinkedIn request, asking for a favor, and hoping for a response. Instead, it's about fostering authentic, two-way relationships where both parties are invested in each other's success. In the world of startups, relationships that are built on genuine interest, respect, and collaboration are the ones that tend to endure, creating long-term opportunities for both you and the people you meet.

Start thinking about networking as a process of relationship-building, not just a way to collect contacts. You're looking for partners, mentors, collaborators, and supporters—not just people who can give you a quick favor or introduce you to someone else.

The Power of Mentorship

In the early stages of a startup, mentorship is one of the most valuable resources you can have. A mentor is someone who's been through the grind before, has walked the path you're on, and can offer advice, guidance, and perspective. But finding the right mentor isn't always straightforward.

Mentorship is about building a long-term relationship with someone who is invested in your growth and willing to provide you with their time and wisdom. This relationship doesn't need to be formal—many great mentorships happen informally through conversations, advice over coffee, or sharing experiences.

A mentor is not just someone who gives you business advice. They can offer you guidance on everything—from mental resilience to time management, to strategies for building a successful company culture. A mentor is someone who will challenge you, hold you accountable, and sometimes even provide a fresh perspective when you're feeling stuck.

How to Find the Right Mentor:

1. **Look for experience, not just success:** A mentor doesn't have to be someone who's famous or has had massive success. Look for someone who has experienced the same hurdles you're facing, even if

they've failed or made mistakes along the way. The value of mentorship comes from learning from others' journeys, including their missteps.

2. **Find someone who resonates with your values:** A good mentor is someone who shares or understands your values and vision. This helps ensure that their advice will be aligned with your goals and your startup's mission.

3. **Be open to feedback, even if it's tough:** Mentors should challenge you, not just validate your ideas. Be open to constructive criticism. This will help you grow not only as an entrepreneur but also as a leader.

4. **Make the first move:** Sometimes, it's up to you to reach out to potential mentors. Don't wait for them to come to you. Send a thoughtful message or invitation for a casual coffee chat. Be genuine, and explain why you think they could offer you valuable

insights. Be specific about what you hope to learn, and show a willingness to invest in the relationship.

Networking with Purpose

Traditional networking can feel shallow at times. We've all been to events where it seems like people are just swapping business cards without ever making a real connection. This kind of networking, while common, is often unproductive.

Instead, aim to network with purpose. When you attend events or interact with others, think about what you can offer in return. How can you help others? What value can you bring to the table? This approach shifts your mindset from "What can I get from this?" to "How can I build something of value together?"

Keys to Purposeful Networking:

1. **Be authentic:** People are good at detecting when someone is being insincere or self-serving. Avoid trying to be someone you're not. Be

yourself, and be genuinely interested in the people you meet.

2. **Focus on building trust:** Building trust is key to any relationship. Don't expect instant outcomes. Trust is developed over time through consistent communication, delivering on promises, and being reliable.

3. **Offer value first:** Rather than immediately asking for something, consider how you can add value to the other person's life. Offer your expertise, share relevant resources, or connect them with someone in your network who might be helpful. By helping others first, you set the foundation for meaningful reciprocity.

4. **Follow up:** After meeting someone new, always follow up. A quick thank-you message or note expressing appreciation for the conversation goes a long way. This is how you transition from a one-time interaction to a long-term relationship.

Building Your Network in the Right Spaces

Networking doesn't always have to happen at formal events. There are countless places to find and connect with others who share your interests and values. Start by identifying the spaces where like-minded entrepreneurs, investors, or mentors gather.

- **Startup Events and Conferences:** These are great opportunities to meet people who are also passionate about building businesses. But don't just go to "network"—go to learn, connect, and build relationships.

- **Online Communities:** Platforms like LinkedIn, Twitter, or startup-focused forums can be excellent places to build relationships. Engage in discussions, share useful insights, and join relevant groups where you can connect with others in your industry.

- **Industry Meetups:** Look for local meetups or community events in your city that focus on entrepreneurship or your specific industry. These informal settings often lead to more meaningful connections.

- **Advisory Boards and Panels:** Many successful entrepreneurs and professionals volunteer their time on advisory boards for startups. Reaching out to individuals involved in these boards can be an excellent way to find mentors and advisors who are willing to share their experience.

Creating a Network of Mutual Support

Building your network is not just about adding people to your contact list—it's about creating a system of support. A great network is one where everyone is invested in helping each other. You may not always have immediate answers or solutions, but if you cultivate an environment of collaboration, people will always be willing to help when you need it.

This mutual support system can offer more than just business advice—it can provide emotional support when things get tough.

Entrepreneurs face many challenges, and having a network of trusted people who understand the unique pressures of building a startup can be incredibly valuable for your mental and emotional well-being.

The Long-Term Value of Relationships

As your startup grows, so will your relationships. The connections you make early on can turn into partnerships, collaborations, and even friendships that last for years. These relationships become part of your entrepreneurial journey, and over time, the people you've built meaningful connections with will play a pivotal role in your success.

In the world of startups, no one succeeds alone. Relationships are the fuel that will propel your business forward. The key to success isn't just in the product you build, but in the people you connect with and surround yourself with.

Book Recommendation:

"Give and Take: Why Helping Others Drives Our Success" by Adam Grant
This book challenges the traditional idea of networking, offering a fresh perspective on how giving can lead to receiving. It emphasizes the power of creating genuine relationships based on generosity, collaboration, and mutual support, which is exactly the kind of networking that can help your startup thrive. Whether you're looking for mentors, customers, or partners, Grant's insights will help you build a network that supports your startup's growth and long-term success.

Chapter 12: Growth Hacks – Scaling Your Startup Fast with Minimal Resources

In the early stages of your startup, resources are often scarce. You may have limited funding, a small team, and a long list of things to do. But that doesn't mean you can't scale quickly. The secret to scaling without a massive budget lies in the power of growth hacks—creative, low-cost strategies that help you reach your audience and achieve significant growth with minimal resources.

In this chapter, we'll explore some of the most effective growth hacking strategies that can help you achieve fast growth in a resource-constrained environment. These strategies are all about working smarter, not harder, and leveraging what you already have to get maximum impact.

What is Growth Hacking?

Growth hacking is a term that originated in the startup world, and it's all about experimenting with different marketing tactics, strategies, and product tweaks to find the fastest and most efficient ways to grow your business. The key idea is to achieve exponential growth without relying on traditional, high-cost methods like large-scale advertising campaigns or hiring a massive team.

Growth hacks can include everything from viral marketing campaigns to product tweaks that increase conversion rates. It's about trying new things, testing rapidly, and doubling down on what works. As a founder with limited resources, growth hacking is one of the most powerful tools in your arsenal.

The Mindset Behind Growth Hacking

To make growth hacking work, you need to adopt the right mindset. It's not about having a big budget or a perfect plan; it's about creativity, experimentation, and being resourceful. You need to be willing to try new things, fail quickly, and pivot when something doesn't work.

Think of growth hacking as a continuous loop of testing and iterating. You try different ideas, measure the results, and refine your approach based on what works. The key to growth hacking is not being afraid to experiment—because even failures can lead to valuable insights that shape your next steps.

1. Leverage Social Proof

People trust what other people say. Social proof is one of the most powerful growth hacks, especially for startups with minimal resources. Social proof can come in many forms: customer reviews, testimonials, influencer endorsements, and case studies.

When you're just starting out, try to get your first users to share their experiences on social media or write testimonials for your product. You can even offer incentives for them to do so, like discounts or freebies. The key is to create trust and build momentum by showing potential customers that others have had a positive experience with your product.

Here are a few strategies you can use:

- **User-Generated Content (UGC):** Encourage your customers to create content (photos, videos, reviews) showcasing your product. UGC not only provides social proof but also acts as free marketing.

- **Influencer Marketing on a Budget:** You don't need to pay big-name influencers to see results. Look for micro-influencers in your niche who are willing to work with you for free products or smaller fees. Their smaller but highly engaged following can drive more meaningful results.

- **Customer Testimonials:** Collect feedback from your earliest customers and use their testimonials in your marketing materials. Real, authentic reviews are highly effective in convincing others to give your product a try.

2. Referral Programs

Referral programs are one of the most cost-effective ways to grow quickly. Essentially, you're turning your existing customers into your most powerful salespeople by incentivizing them to refer others. When executed properly, a referral program can lead to viral growth.

Referral programs work best when you provide value to both the referrer and the referee. For example, offering discounts, free products, or exclusive access to new features can motivate your customers to spread the word. Many companies, such as Dropbox and Airbnb, grew rapidly with the help of simple but effective referral programs.

Here are some tips for creating an effective referral program:

- **Make the rewards clear and valuable:** Offer rewards that are appealing enough to incentivize your customers to refer others. These could be discounts, free products, or exclusive access to new features.

- **Keep it simple:** The referral process should be easy to understand and simple to execute. Provide your customers with unique links or codes they can share with their friends.

- **Track everything:** Use referral tracking software to monitor the effectiveness of your program and see who's referring the most people.

3. Viral Loops and Contests

A viral loop is a marketing strategy where your existing users drive new users into your system. It's a simple, yet highly effective, growth hack that leverages word-of-mouth marketing. Contests and giveaways are a great way to generate buzz and create a viral loop.

To create a viral loop, you need to make it easy for users to invite others to join your platform. You can offer a reward for every referral or provide a special incentive for those who refer the most people.

Here's how you can create a viral loop using contests:

- **Create shareable contests:** Offer prizes that resonate with your audience (e.g., free products, cash prizes, exclusive access). Make it easy for users to participate and share with their friends.

- **Leverage social sharing:** Ask users to share the contest on their social media profiles or invite friends to enter in exchange for extra entries or rewards. The more people who enter, the more exposure your business gets.

- **Keep the prize valuable:** To drive participation, the prize should be desirable and relevant to your target market.

4. Leverage Free Tools and Platforms

One of the biggest advantages startups have over larger companies is agility. While big companies may need a large marketing budget to get noticed, you can take advantage of free tools and platforms to grow your business without spending a dime.

Here are some ways to leverage free tools to accelerate growth:

- **Social Media:** Use social media platforms like Instagram, Twitter, LinkedIn, and TikTok to engage with your audience and build a community around your brand. Consistent, high-quality content can help you build momentum without spending any money on advertising.

- **Content Marketing:** Create valuable, informative content that can help solve your audience's problems. Start a blog, create YouTube videos, or use podcasts to engage with your audience and drive organic traffic.

- **SEO:** Search Engine Optimization (SEO) is a long-term strategy, but it can drive organic traffic to your website without spending money on ads. Focus on creating high-quality content that addresses the needs and interests of your target audience.

- **Email Marketing:** Use free tools like Mailchimp or Sendinblue to grow your email list and nurture relationships with your customers. Email marketing is one of the most cost-effective ways to drive repeat business and engage with your audience.

5. Optimize Your Product for Growth

A growth hack doesn't always have to be a marketing tactic. Sometimes, the best way to scale is by optimizing your product itself. By designing a product with built-in growth mechanisms, you can ensure that every customer you acquire becomes a potential advocate for your brand.

Here are a few ways to optimize your product for growth:

- **Make it easy for users to share your product:** Incorporate features that make it easy for your users to recommend your product to their friends (e.g., sharing buttons, referral programs, social media integrations).

- **Create an unforgettable user experience:** If your product is exceptional, users will talk about it. Ensure that your product is not only functional but delightful to use.

- **Encourage user-generated content:** Give users the ability to easily create and share content related to your product (e.g., user-generated reviews, photos, and videos).

6. Content Partnerships

Collaborating with other brands or influencers in your niche can help you reach a broader audience without a significant investment. Content partnerships, such as guest blogging, co-hosting webinars, or cross-promoting on social media, allow you to tap into someone else's audience and increase your brand's visibility.

When looking for potential partners, find those whose audience aligns with yours but is not in direct competition with you. The goal is to create a win-win situation where both parties benefit from increased exposure and value.

Book Recommendation:

"Growth Hacker Marketing: A Primer on the Future of PR, Marketing, and Advertising" by Ryan Holiday
This book is a must-read for anyone looking to master the art of growth hacking. Ryan

Holiday breaks down the core principles of growth hacking and shows how startups can leverage creative, low-cost strategies to grow quickly. It's a perfect read for entrepreneurs looking to scale their business on a tight budget and work smarter, not harder.

Chapter 13: Cash Flow and Budgeting – Keeping Your Startup Financially Healthy

For many startup founders, dealing with numbers feels like a foreign language. Financial spreadsheets can look like a series of jumbled figures, and the thought of cash flow and budgeting might make you break out in a cold sweat. But here's the hard truth: if you don't get a handle on your finances, your business could struggle or, worse, fail.

You don't need to be a financial expert to succeed as a founder, but you do need to be financially literate enough to keep your startup healthy. In this chapter, we'll break down cash flow and budgeting in a way that's simple, practical, and relevant to your business—without the jargon.

Let's take the fear out of finance and make it work for you.

What is Cash Flow, and Why Does it Matter?

Cash flow is the lifeblood of your business. In simple terms, it's the movement of money into and out of your business. If cash is flowing in faster than it's flowing out, you're in the clear. If it's the other way around, you could face serious problems—like being unable to pay suppliers, employees, or your rent.

For many early-stage startups, cash flow is unpredictable. You may go through phases of feast (when sales are booming) and famine (when sales drop or you're waiting for payments). Cash flow management is about making sure you have enough money to cover your essential costs at all times, even during lean periods.

Here's why cash flow is crucial:

- **It ensures you can pay bills on time:** Delayed payments to suppliers, vendors, and contractors can harm relationships and hurt your business reputation.

- **It helps avoid financial panic:** If you know where your money is coming from and where it's going, you'll avoid those moments of panic when you wonder if you can make payroll.

- **It keeps you sustainable:** Cash flow helps you navigate fluctuations in revenue, ensuring that you can keep operating in the short term while planning for growth.

Understanding Cash Flow Basics

While cash flow may sound like a complicated concept, there are really just three main components you need to focus on:

1. **Cash Inflows (Income):** This is the money coming into your business. It includes revenue from product sales, investments, loans, and any other income.

2. **Cash Outflows (Expenses):** This is the money going out. It includes rent, salaries, marketing costs, operational expenses, inventory purchases, etc.

3. **Net Cash Flow:** This is simply the difference between your cash inflows and outflows. Positive cash flow means you're bringing in more money than you're spending, and negative

cash flow means you're running at a loss.

The goal is to consistently monitor and manage these numbers to keep your business financially healthy.

Common Cash Flow Mistakes to Avoid

1. **Ignoring Cash Flow Projections:** One of the biggest mistakes new founders make is thinking that cash flow will just take care of itself. It won't. Always project your cash flow, so you know when you're going to have more money and when you might have a shortage. This helps you avoid surprises.

2. **Not Accounting for Delayed Payments:** Many startups operate on a payment structure where customers pay on terms (e.g., net 30 days). That means you may not receive your payment for weeks after providing your product or service. Always account for these delays in your cash flow projections.

3. **Underestimating Operational Costs:** The costs of running a business can pile up quickly, especially in the early stages when you're trying to scale. It's easy to underestimate how much things like marketing, salaries, and overhead will cost. Always leave room in your budget for unexpected expenses.

4. **Mixing Personal and Business Finances:** As tempting as it might be to combine your personal and business accounts when you're starting out, it's a huge mistake. You need to keep them separate for a clear view of your business's financial health. This will also make things much easier come tax time.

Budgeting – The Art of Planning for the Future

Now that you understand the importance of cash flow, let's dive into budgeting. While cash flow looks at what's happening in real-time, budgeting is about planning for the future. A good budget is the foundation of a healthy financial plan.

As a startup, your budget will be the roadmap to help you allocate resources efficiently, stay on track, and ensure that you're using your money wisely. Here's how to build a budget that works for your business:

1. Track Your Income and Expenses

The first step in creating a budget is understanding where your money comes from and where it goes. This means tracking all sources of income (sales, investments, etc.) and listing out every expense (rent, salaries, marketing, supplies, etc.).

This doesn't need to be a complex system. You can use a simple spreadsheet or budgeting tools like QuickBooks or Wave to track these. The key is to make sure you're accounting for everything. Missing just a few expenses can cause your budget to be off and lead to unnecessary cash flow problems.

2. Categorize Your Expenses

Expenses can be broken down into two categories:

- **Fixed Expenses:** These are expenses that are consistent each month, like rent, utilities, and salaries. They don't change much, so they're easier to predict.

- **Variable Expenses:** These are expenses that change based on factors like sales volume, raw material costs, or marketing spending. For example, if you spend more on marketing to increase sales, your variable expenses will rise.

A smart budgeting approach involves separating these categories, so you can track fixed expenses that you can count on, and variable expenses that fluctuate depending on your business activity.

3. Set Financial Goals

One of the best ways to stay motivated and on track is by setting financial goals. These goals will help guide your spending and savings decisions. For example, you might set goals for:

- **Revenue targets:** How much revenue do you want to generate in a given quarter or year?

- **Profitability goals:** At what point do you want to become profitable? What's your target profit margin?

- **Savings goals:** How much money should be in the bank to cover unexpected costs?

Having financial goals will keep you focused and help you measure your progress.

4. Monitor and Adjust Regularly

A budget isn't set in stone. It's a living document that needs to be revisited and adjusted regularly. As your business grows, your expenses and income streams will evolve. Regularly monitor your budget and cash flow to make adjustments as needed. The more you track and adjust, the better you'll get at predicting financial outcomes and avoiding surprises.

5. Prioritize Spending

As a founder, you will face constant pressure to spend money on various aspects of your business. The key is to prioritize spending that will yield the highest return. For example, investing in marketing that brings in new customers is likely more valuable than buying expensive office furniture.

Ask yourself: **"Will this investment directly contribute to the growth of my business?"**

If not, consider holding off until you have more capital or until it's absolutely necessary.

Creative Tips for Managing Cash Flow on a Tight Budget

1. **Negotiate with Vendors:** Don't be afraid to negotiate payment terms with vendors. Ask for discounts for paying early or extended terms to give yourself more time to pay.

2. **Leverage Crowdfunding or Pre-Sales:** Platforms like Kickstarter or Indiegogo can give you cash flow before you even produce your

product. This can help fund initial production without having to go into debt.

3. **Automate Payments:** Use automated tools for recurring payments like subscriptions or monthly bills to prevent missed deadlines and late fees.

4. **Track Your Metrics:** Make sure to track your key metrics like customer acquisition cost (CAC), lifetime value (LTV), and churn rate. These numbers help you make more informed decisions about where to allocate resources.

Conclusion: Stay Financially Healthy, Stay in the Game

Cash flow and budgeting are the backbone of a financially healthy startup. As a founder, you need to be comfortable with managing your numbers, even if you don't love them. If you stay on top of cash flow, track your spending, and stick to a realistic budget, your business will be much better positioned for growth and sustainability.

Remember, a startup isn't a sprint; it's a marathon. And to run that marathon, you need a solid financial foundation to support you along the way. Start simple, stay disciplined, and as your business grows, you'll gain a deeper understanding of your finances—without the panic.

Book Recommendation:

"The Lean CFO: Architect of the Lean Management System" by Nicholas S. Katko

This book is perfect for startup founders who want to understand the financial aspects of their business in a practical, actionable way. It's particularly useful for founders who are just beginning to grasp the importance of cash flow and budgeting. The Lean CFO will teach you how to manage your financial resources effectively while growing your startup.

Chapter 14: Building Your Brand Identity – Creating a Memorable Startup Brand

Your brand is more than just a logo or a name on a product. It's the entire experience that people have with your company—the way they feel when they hear your name, see your product, or interact with your business. Building a strong brand identity is essential for standing out in a crowded marketplace and connecting deeply with your audience.

In this chapter, we'll explore how to create a memorable brand identity that not only resonates with your target customers but also helps you build a loyal community around your startup. Whether you're just starting out or looking to refine your existing brand, the strategies and principles here will guide you in the right direction.

What is Brand Identity?

Brand identity is the combination of visual, verbal, and emotional elements that define your brand. It's the way you communicate with your customers, the image you present to the world, and the promise you make about who you are and what you stand for.

A strong brand identity makes your company recognizable, trustworthy, and relevant. It helps customers connect with your mission, values, and products on a deeper level. In essence, your brand identity should be the personality of your business, shining through everything you do.

Why is Brand Identity Important?

1. **Differentiation:** A strong brand identity helps you stand out in a competitive market. It tells customers why your product or service is unique, and why they should care.

2. **Trust and Loyalty:** Customers are more likely to trust and return to a brand that they can recognize and relate to. A consistent and compelling brand identity creates a sense of reliability and trustworthiness.

3. **Emotional Connection:** A well-crafted brand identity connects with customers on an emotional level, making them feel like they're part of

something bigger than just a product or service.

4. **Consistency:** Consistency across all touchpoints—whether it's your website, social media, packaging, or customer service—helps reinforce your brand's message and makes it easier for customers to recognize and remember you.

Key Elements of Brand Identity

Let's break down the key elements you need to focus on when building your brand identity:

1. Brand Vision and Mission

Your **brand vision** is your long-term goal—the bigger picture of what you want to achieve with your brand. It's the reason your company exists beyond making a profit.

Your **brand mission** is how you plan to achieve that vision. It defines the core purpose of your business and the impact you aim to have on your customers or the world.

Example:
If your brand is all about sustainability, your mission might be to create eco-friendly products that help reduce waste. Your vision could be to create a world where sustainability is the norm, not the exception.

Tip: Ensure that your vision and mission are not just words on a page but something that resonates with your target audience. This will help them connect with your brand on a deeper level.

2. Brand Values

Brand values are the guiding principles that shape the behavior of your company. They're what you stand for and believe in. These values influence your decisions, your culture, and the way you interact with customers.

Examples of brand values include:

- **Authenticity:** Being genuine and transparent in all dealings.
- **Innovation:** Continuously striving to offer new and better solutions.

- **Sustainability:** Committing to environmentally-friendly practices.
- **Empathy:** Understanding and catering to the needs and desires of your customers.

Tip: Your brand values should align with the expectations and beliefs of your target audience. If your values don't resonate with your customers, it'll be harder to build lasting relationships.

3. Brand Personality

Just like people, brands have personalities. Your brand's personality is shaped by the tone, voice, and overall vibe that you communicate to your audience. Is your brand playful and fun? Or serious and professional? Maybe it's bold and rebellious? The personality you choose should reflect both your business values and your target audience's preferences.

Example:
If your target market is young, creative individuals, your brand personality might be bold, playful, and energetic, while a brand

targeting professionals might have a more refined and sophisticated tone.

Tip: Keep your brand's personality consistent across all channels. Whether it's your social media posts, website copy, or customer service, the personality you project should feel like a coherent reflection of your brand.

4. Visual Identity – Logo, Colors, and Typography

The visual elements of your brand—such as your **logo**, **color palette**, and **typography**—are the first things people see. These elements are crucial in making a strong, lasting impression.

- **Logo:** Your logo should be simple, memorable, and aligned with your brand's values. It's the face of your brand and will be used on everything from your website to your product packaging.

- **Color Palette:** Colors evoke emotions and can communicate certain messages. For example, blue often conveys trust and professionalism, while red can signify energy and excitement. Choose colors that align with the emotions you want your brand to evoke.

- **Typography:** The fonts you choose should be readable, but also reflect your brand personality. If you're a luxury brand, you might opt for a sleek, elegant font, while a fun, youthful brand might go for something bold and quirky.

Tip: Keep it simple and make sure your visual identity is consistent across all touchpoints. If someone sees your logo, they should instantly know it's your brand.

5. Brand Voice and Messaging

Your **brand voice** is how you communicate with your audience through words. It's influenced by your brand's personality and is reflected in everything from your social media posts to email campaigns and advertisements.

Some brands opt for a professional, formal voice, while others may use humor or be more casual and conversational. Your messaging should always resonate with your target audience and reflect your brand values.

Tip: Establish clear guidelines for your brand voice to ensure consistency across all platforms. Whether you're writing a blog post, posting on Instagram, or replying to customer emails, your voice should remain coherent.

Crafting a Brand Story

Humans are hardwired to connect with stories. One of the most powerful ways to build your brand identity is to craft a compelling **brand story**—the narrative that explains who you are, where you've come from, and why you do what you do.

Your brand story doesn't have to be complex, but it should convey:

- **Your origin:** Where did you start? What inspired you to create this brand?

- **Your challenges:** What obstacles have you overcome to get where you are now?
- **Your impact:** What do you hope to achieve with your brand? How will you change lives or the world?
- **Your vision for the future:** Where do you see your brand in the years to come?

A great brand story makes customers feel like they're part of your journey. It builds loyalty and creates a deeper emotional connection with your audience.

Consistency is Key

One of the most important things to remember when building your brand identity is that **consistency is key**. Your brand identity should be reflected consistently across all touchpoints—your website, social media, packaging, emails, customer service, and even in-person interactions.

When your brand is consistent, it builds recognition, trust, and reliability. Customers know what to expect from your brand, and they can easily identify you among the competition.

Tips for Building a Memorable Brand Identity

1. **Know Your Audience:** The first step in building a memorable brand is understanding who your audience is. What are their pain points? What do they care about? What kind of brands do they already love and why? The better you understand them, the better you can build a brand that resonates.

2. **Be Authentic:** Authenticity is crucial for building trust. Don't try to be something you're not. Be true to your values, vision, and what you stand for, and your audience will connect with you on a deeper level.

3. **Deliver Value:** Your brand isn't just about how it looks or sounds. It's about the value you provide to your customers. Always prioritize delivering an excellent product or

service that aligns with your brand promise.

4. **Stand for Something:** Don't be afraid to take a stand on issues that matter to your brand. Whether it's social responsibility, environmental sustainability, or innovation, standing for something gives your brand purpose and makes it more memorable.

Book Recommendation:

"Building a StoryBrand: Clarify Your Message So Customers Will Listen" by Donald Miller

This book offers a practical guide to creating a powerful and clear brand message that resonates with customers. By focusing on the story you tell, you'll learn how to build a brand identity that connects deeply with your audience and drives business growth.

Chapter 15: Leadership and Team Building – How to Lead During the Growth Phase

Leadership isn't about dictating orders or maintaining a position of power—it's about guiding your team with purpose, vision, and empathy. As your startup moves into the growth phase, how you lead will shape the culture of your company, impact team morale, and drive long-term success.

In this chapter, we'll explore what it means to be a leader during the growth stage of your business, with an emphasis on empathy, authenticity, and inspiring your team to achieve their best work. Leadership during this stage is less about traditional authority and more about fostering collaboration, trust, and a sense of shared mission.

Leading with Empathy

In the early stages of a startup, everyone is usually involved in every decision, every task. As you grow, however, you start to delegate more and need to rely on a team of individuals to bring your vision to life. That means you'll need to lean into empathetic leadership.

Empathy is the ability to understand and share the feelings of another. As a leader, it's about recognizing the struggles and aspirations of your team and supporting them through those challenges. In the growth phase, empathy is crucial because it ensures that the team remains motivated, engaged, and aligned with the company's goals.

Why Empathy Matters

- **Builds Trust:** When employees feel understood, they trust you more. This trust leads to more open communication, better feedback, and a stronger sense of loyalty.

- **Improves Morale:** A leader who shows empathy acknowledges the human side of work—people need to feel valued, respected, and understood. A positive atmosphere leads to greater productivity and less turnover.

- **Fosters Collaboration:** Empathetic leaders are better equipped to handle conflict, mediate issues, and ensure that everyone feels heard.

When team members feel that their voices matter, they're more likely to collaborate and work toward shared goals.

Tip: Practice active listening, where you fully concentrate, understand, and respond thoughtfully to what your team is saying. This builds connection and helps create an open line of communication.

Leading with Authenticity

Authenticity is an essential part of leadership that's often overlooked. Authentic leaders lead with honesty, integrity, and a clear sense of who they are. They don't try to be someone they're not to impress others—they own their decisions, admit when they're wrong, and stand by their values.

Being authentic means being true to yourself and your values, and that resonates with your team. As your company grows, people will look to you not just for business direction but for inspiration. If you present a façade that's inconsistent with your true self, it will cause confusion, mistrust, and disconnect. When you lead with authenticity, your team feels comfortable doing the same, which fosters an open and inclusive culture.

Why Authenticity Matters

- **Attracts and Retains Talent:** Authentic leaders build genuine connections with their teams, which makes them more likely to attract passionate and aligned talent. Team members stay with a leader they believe in.

- **Drives Consistency:** When your values, actions, and communication are aligned, you create a sense of stability for your team. Consistency in leadership sets the tone for how employees should interact with one another and how they should represent the brand.

- **Promotes Trust:** People follow leaders they trust. Authenticity builds trust by showing your team that you are who you say you are, and your actions match your words.

Tip: Be open about your mistakes and challenges. Admitting that you don't have all the answers shows vulnerability and humanizes you as a leader.

Setting the Vision and Direction

As your startup grows, one of your most important roles as a leader is to set the vision and direction. This isn't just about creating a business plan and leaving it there—it's about actively communicating your vision, aligning your team with it, and inspiring them to bring it to life.

In the growth phase, your startup is likely facing bigger challenges, expanding into new markets, or scaling operations. The team will look to you for guidance and clarity on how to move forward. If they understand the "why" behind what they're doing, they'll be more motivated to take action.

Why Vision Matters

- **Provides Clarity:** A well-articulated vision tells the team where the company is headed and why it matters. It helps team members understand their roles in the bigger picture and gives them a sense of purpose.

- **Drives Engagement:** When people are connected to a vision that excites them, they are more likely to stay engaged and contribute their best efforts. A sense of purpose leads to higher motivation and creativity.

- **Aligns the Team:** A clear vision ensures that everyone is on the same page, working toward the same goals. It minimizes confusion and allows team members to make decisions with the company's long-term success in mind.

Tip: Regularly communicate the vision, not just through official meetings but in day-to-day interactions. Make sure the vision is present in everything you do—your actions should reflect your words.

Building a Strong and Diverse Team

Great leaders know that they cannot succeed alone. The growth phase is when you start to build a team that will help you scale. Whether you're hiring your first employees or bringing on contractors, it's crucial to focus on building a team that supports your company's vision and culture.

Why Team Building Matters

- **Leverage Different Strengths:** A diverse team brings a variety of perspectives, ideas, and skill sets. The more diverse your team, the more likely you are to find creative solutions to challenges and adapt to changes quickly.

- **Shared Accountability:** When you hire people who are aligned with your values and vision, everyone works together to achieve the same goals. This collective responsibility makes everyone more invested in the company's success.

- **Culture is Everything:** The people you hire will shape your company's culture. As a leader, you must be intentional about the kind of team you want to build. Focus on finding individuals who are passionate, innovative, and collaborative.

Tip: Hire for cultural fit first, and then look for technical skills. A great cultural fit ensures that your team will work well together, even when faced with challenges.

Developing Your Leadership Skills

The best leaders are always working to improve themselves. Leading a growing team means evolving as a leader and learning new skills. Whether it's improving your communication, decision-making, or conflict resolution skills, always be open to feedback and self-reflection.

How to Develop Leadership Skills

- **Seek Feedback:** Don't be afraid to ask your team for feedback on your leadership style. This shows that you value their input and are committed to improving.

- **Mentorship:** Seek out mentors who can guide you through difficult situations and help you grow as a leader. Learning from others who have gone through similar experiences is invaluable.

- **Invest in Learning:** Read books, attend workshops, and surround yourself with leaders who inspire you. Growth as a leader comes from continual learning.

Tip: Practice self-awareness. Reflect on your strengths and weaknesses as a leader, and actively work on areas that need improvement.

Leading Through Challenges

In the growth phase, your startup will inevitably face challenges—whether it's a sudden drop in sales, a product failure, or a leadership crisis. As a leader, how you handle these challenges sets the tone for the entire company.

- **Stay Calm and Collected:** Your team looks to you for reassurance during times of crisis. If you panic, they will panic. Stay calm, think strategically, and communicate clearly.

- **Embrace Adaptability:** Growth doesn't come without turbulence. Be ready to pivot when necessary, and encourage your team to adapt to new circumstances.

- **Inspire Perseverance:** Your team will follow your lead. Show them that setbacks are just learning opportunities, and encourage them to keep pushing forward.

Tip: Focus on the long-term vision even when immediate circumstances are challenging. Helping your team stay focused on the bigger picture will keep them motivated through tough times.

Book Recommendation:

"Leaders Eat Last: Why Some Teams Pull Together and Others Don't" by Simon Sinek
This book dives into the concept of leadership from a human-centered perspective, emphasizing the importance of trust, empathy, and strong relationships within teams. Sinek explores how great

leaders inspire loyalty and cooperation, focusing on the fundamental principles that can guide you in leading your team during the growth phase.

Chapter 16: The Pivot – When and How to Change Course Without Losing Momentum

In the world of startups, the ability to pivot is one of the most crucial skills you can develop. Not every plan works as expected. The market may change, customer needs might evolve, or new challenges could arise that force you to reconsider your approach. A pivot isn't a failure—it's a strategic shift that keeps your business moving forward in the right direction.

In this chapter, we'll dive into the art of pivoting, exploring when it's time to change course, how to execute a pivot smoothly, and how to keep your startup's momentum intact. Pivoting doesn't mean abandoning your vision; it means adapting to new realities in a way that strengthens your foundation rather than weakening it.

Recognizing When a Pivot is Needed

The first step in pivoting is knowing when it's time to change direction. It's not always obvious, and sometimes it requires a shift in mindset. Here are a few signs that it may be time for a pivot:

1. Customer Feedback Is Telling You Something Different

Your customers are your best resource for understanding the direction of your product or service. If you're hearing consistent feedback that your offering isn't meeting their needs or they're not interested in it, it may be time to reassess. A pivot could mean adjusting your product, finding a new customer base, or even changing your pricing structure.

Example: A company that initially started offering a physical fitness app but realized users were more interested in the nutritional side of health might pivot to focus entirely on nutrition.

2. The Market Is Changing Faster Than Your Product

If you're unable to keep up with industry trends or a new competitor emerges with a more compelling offering, your current path may not be sustainable. Keeping an eye on market shifts is essential for spotting opportunities to pivot early.

Example: A startup that initially launched as a software-only solution but finds increasing demand for mobile apps might pivot to include mobile app functionality to stay competitive.

3. Your Business Isn't Scaling as Expected

If you're hitting roadblocks in terms of growth—whether it's customer acquisition, revenue generation, or operational limitations—it's a sign that your business model or approach may need to change. Pivoting can help you break through these barriers and uncover a more scalable path.

Example: A company struggling to scale its direct-to-consumer model might pivot to a B2B model, targeting businesses instead of individual consumers.

4. You're Not Passionate About the Current Direction

Sometimes, the most important sign that it's time to pivot is a gut feeling that the current path isn't right for you as a founder. If you're no longer passionate or motivated by the work you're doing, it can affect your energy, creativity, and leadership.

Example: A founder who initially launched a business in a market they thought was lucrative, but now finds their passion elsewhere, may pivot toward a new business model or product they feel more connected to.

5. Financial Struggles

When revenue projections are not being met, and you find yourself burning through cash reserves faster than expected, it's time to ask hard questions about whether your approach is sustainable. Financial difficulties often highlight the need for a pivot.

Example: A subscription-based service that's unable to attract enough subscribers might pivot toward a one-time purchase model to boost cash flow and reduce ongoing customer acquisition costs.

How to Pivot Without Losing Momentum

Changing direction in business can feel like starting over, but the key to a successful pivot is making the transition as seamless as possible. The last thing you want is to lose the momentum you've built so far. Here's how to pivot strategically without losing speed.

1. Assess Your Core Strengths and Values

Before making a drastic change, identify what your business does best. What are the key strengths that have helped you reach this point? These could be aspects like customer relationships, your technology, brand reputation, or unique expertise. Your pivot should incorporate these core strengths to build on what you've already accomplished.

Example: If your brand has built a loyal customer base around a certain product, consider how you can pivot within that niche or area of expertise, rather than abandoning everything entirely.

2. Communicate the Pivot Clearly

Whether it's your team, your investors, or your customers, everyone involved needs to understand why the pivot is happening and what the new direction looks like.

Transparency is key to maintaining trust and ensuring everyone is aligned.

- **To your team:** Be clear about why the pivot is necessary and how it aligns with the company's vision. A well-informed and motivated team is essential for executing a pivot successfully.

- **To your customers:** If your product or service is changing, it's important to communicate that to your existing customers. Explain how the new direction will benefit them and why the change is a positive one.

- **To your investors:** Make sure your investors understand why the pivot is happening and how it will help the company achieve sustainable growth. They're more likely to continue supporting you if they see that you have a clear plan and rationale.

3. Focus on a Smaller, More Targeted Audience

Pivoting often means narrowing your focus, which can help you streamline your efforts and resources. Instead of trying to serve everyone, target a smaller, more defined customer base with a solution that truly addresses their needs.

Example: If you initially tried to serve a broad market but found that one specific demographic is more interested in your product, pivot to serve that group more effectively. Specializing can help you better tailor your marketing, product features, and customer support.

4. Leverage Your Existing Resources

A successful pivot doesn't require you to throw everything away and start from scratch. Look at the resources you have—your team, technology, customer relationships, brand equity—and figure out how to repurpose or refocus them toward your new direction.

Example: If you've developed a powerful piece of technology for your product, consider how you can apply that technology in a different industry or use case that's more aligned with market demand.

5. Iterate and Test Quickly

Once you've pivoted, it's important to test the new direction as quickly as possible. Launch small-scale tests, gather feedback, and use that data to make rapid iterations. The quicker you learn what works and what doesn't, the faster you can refine your approach and gain momentum.

Example: If you've pivoted to a new product feature, release it to a small group of users first. Gather feedback, analyze the results, and make improvements before a full-scale launch.

6. Stay Flexible and Open to Further Change

A pivot doesn't guarantee immediate success, and it's likely that more changes will be required down the line. Stay flexible and open to further refinement. The key is to keep moving forward and learning from the results of your pivot, rather than clinging to your original vision if it's not working.

Example: After your initial pivot, you may realize that there's still a better way to serve your target market. Stay open to making further adjustments based on new insights and data.

Keeping Momentum After a Pivot

It's easy to feel like a pivot is a step backward, but it's important to maintain momentum in the face of change. Here's how to keep the energy up:

- **Celebrate Small Wins:** After making a pivot, celebrate the small victories along the way. These could be customer sign-ups, new partnerships, or positive feedback on your new direction. These wins build confidence and motivation.

- **Stay Focused on the Big Picture:** While pivots often require short-term changes, always keep the long-term vision in mind. Revisit your mission and goals to remind yourself and your team of the larger purpose behind your work.

- **Maintain a Growth Mindset:** Understand that a pivot is a natural part of the startup journey. View it as an opportunity for growth, learning, and adaptation rather than as a failure. Embrace the uncertainty and see where it leads.

Book Recommendation:

A great book recommendation that dives into the story of a startup pivoting is **"Rework" by Jason Fried and David Heinemeier Hansson**. While the book doesn't focus on one single pivot, it presents numerous real-life examples of how the founders of Basecamp pivoted their business strategy multiple times. It provides a fresh perspective on entrepreneurship, focusing on simplicity, adaptability, and making smart, often counterintuitive decisions—elements crucial when deciding to pivot.

Another excellent choice is **"The Everything Store: Jeff Bezos and the Age of Amazon" by Brad Stone**. The book chronicles how Amazon pivoted several times in its early days—from a bookstore to an e-commerce giant—highlighting the strategic decisions that led to its enormous success. It's a fantastic case study in how recognizing the need to pivot and executing it effectively can shape a startup's future.

Both of these books offer compelling insights into how a startup can pivot successfully while maintaining focus and long-term vision.

Chapter 17: Scaling Your Product – The Art of Expanding Your Offerings

Scaling a product is one of the most exciting yet daunting stages of a startup journey. You've proven your idea works, you've found some traction, and now it's time to think about expanding. But scaling isn't about blindly adding new products or services. It's about doing so with purpose—ensuring that each new offering aligns with your brand, addresses market demand, and fits seamlessly into your growth strategy.

In this chapter, we will explore the art of scaling your product offering thoughtfully and strategically. We'll discuss how to expand your product line, refine your existing offerings, and scale at a pace that maintains your company's core values. The key here is balance. You need to grow without losing sight of what makes your startup unique.

1. Understanding Product-Market Fit Before Scaling

Before you even consider scaling, ensure that your current product is solid and that you've reached product-market fit. Simply put, product-market fit is when your offering satisfies a significant demand in the market, and customers are actively purchasing or using it.

Scaling before achieving product-market fit is one of the most common mistakes startups make. If you scale too early, you risk spreading yourself too thin and investing time and money into products that haven't proven themselves yet.

Your product should have a strong customer base, feedback loops that are actionable, and enough operational systems in place to handle growth. If you can meet these prerequisites, then you're ready to start thinking about scaling.

2. How to Scale With Purpose

Scaling without purpose is like building a skyscraper without a solid foundation. If you want your new product offerings to succeed, you need to scale with intention. Here's how to approach scaling your product line:

- **Leverage Customer Feedback**: The best way to scale a product is to listen to your customers. They are the ones who will tell you what they need next. Whether it's through surveys, direct conversations, or analyzing customer behaviors, their feedback is the goldmine that can direct your next steps.

- **Solve an Existing Problem**: When expanding your offerings, make sure your new products solve a problem your current customers face. A logical expansion comes from addressing gaps in your current offering or adding something that complements it. For example, if you sell skincare products, introducing a complementary line like moisturizers or masks makes sense. However, launching a completely unrelated product, like apparel, might not.

- **Align with Your Brand Values**: Your new product should reflect the same values, tone, and mission as your original offering. Scaling with a mismatch in product offerings can confuse your customers and dilute your brand. Your audience trusts your brand because of its consistency, so maintain that trust by scaling in a way that doesn't compromise your core identity.

- **Start Small and Test**: Even if you've hit product-market fit, you don't have to go all in when scaling your product. Start by testing your new offerings with a small segment of your audience. This can be through limited launches, special editions, or even just a pilot version of the product. This allows you to gauge interest, get feedback, and make improvements before a full-scale launch.

3. Ensuring Operational Readiness for Scaling

A critical but often overlooked part of scaling your product is ensuring that your operations can handle the increased demand. This includes supply chain logistics, inventory management, staffing, and customer service. Scaling without thinking about operations can lead to overwhelmed teams, delayed shipments, and poor customer service—issues that can tarnish your hard-earned reputation.

Here are a few operational considerations to ensure you can handle the new products you're adding:

- **Streamline Supply Chain**: As you scale, ensure that your suppliers and manufacturers can keep up with the increased demand. You might need to establish new partnerships, renegotiate contracts, or invest in better technology to streamline your inventory management.

- **Automate When Possible**: As your product offerings grow, look for ways to automate your processes. Whether it's through customer service chatbots, automated email marketing campaigns, or inventory tracking software, automation will free up your time and resources to focus on the creative aspects of scaling your business.

- **Build a Scalable Team**: Scaling also means growing your team. As you expand your product line, consider hiring specialized talent who can help you manage the increased demand. This could include product managers, marketing experts, customer support, or supply chain managers.

4. Marketing Your Expanded Product Line

Marketing plays a significant role when it comes to scaling. As you expand your product offerings, it's essential to ensure your marketing reflects these changes and communicates the value of the new products to your customers.

- **Leverage Existing Channels**: The beauty of scaling is that you already have an established customer base. Use your existing marketing channels—email newsletters, social media, and your website—to introduce your new products. But don't just throw a product launch post out there. Create compelling content that explains why your new products matter and how they fit into your customers' lives.

- **Use Cross-Promotions**: As you introduce new products, cross-promote them with your existing offerings. Bundle deals, upsell opportunities, and loyalty programs are effective ways to generate interest in your new products and drive sales.

- **Influencers and Partnerships**: Collaborating with influencers or like-minded brands is a great way to expand your reach as you scale. They can help you introduce your products to new audiences and add credibility to your brand.

5. Managing the Risk of Overexpansion

As tempting as it is to launch multiple new products, there's a risk of overexpansion. You might be eager to capture a bigger share of the market, but scaling too quickly can spread your resources thin and create operational chaos.

Be mindful of your bandwidth—both in terms of resources and energy. Prioritize the products that are most aligned with your long-term vision and be strategic about the timing of new launches.

Book Recommendation:

For a deeper dive into the art of scaling products thoughtfully, I recommend **"Blitzscaling: The Lightning-Fast Path to Building Massively Valuable Companies" by Reid Hoffman and Chris Yeh.** This book dives into the techniques used by some of the fastest-growing startups and gives practical advice on how to scale rapidly while managing the challenges that come with it. It's perfect for founders looking to accelerate their growth while maintaining a strategic edge.

Chapter 18: Future-Proofing Your Business – Building for Long-Term Success

As a founder, it's easy to get caught up in the daily grind of running your business—the immediate customer needs, the day-to-day operations, and the constant hustle to stay relevant. But what happens once you've achieved some level of success? How do you ensure that your business not only survives the ups and downs of the market but thrives for years to come?

The final chapter is about thinking beyond the present and building a business that is resilient, adaptable, and capable of long-term growth. This is the art of **future-proofing** your business—creating systems, structures, and strategies that ensure your startup will remain competitive, profitable, and sustainable well into the future.

Here's how to start future-proofing your business for long-term success:

1. Building Scalable Systems

A sustainable business isn't built on hustle alone—it's built on solid systems that can scale as your company grows. At the start, you may wear many hats, but as you grow, you need to automate, delegate, and optimize.

- **Automation for Efficiency**: Implement tools and software to automate as many tasks as possible. From customer support bots to automated email marketing and CRM (Customer Relationship Management) systems, automation will save you time and allow you to focus on the more strategic aspects of your business.

- **Streamline Operations**: Simplify processes that allow you to scale easily. This includes inventory management, sales workflows, and order fulfillment systems. The simpler your operations, the easier it will be to scale as you expand to new markets or add more product lines.

- **Data-Driven Decisions**: The future of business is in data. Start collecting and analyzing data on your sales, customer behavior, website traffic, and more. This will help you make informed decisions about product development, marketing strategies, and customer acquisition.

2. Diversifying Revenue Streams

One of the most effective ways to future-proof your business is by **diversifying your revenue streams**. Relying on one source of income—whether it's a single product, a single customer, or one channel—can be risky, especially if there's a shift in market trends or customer preferences. Here are a few ways to diversify:

- **Introduce New Product Lines**: If you've successfully launched one product, consider how you can expand into complementary product lines. This might mean adding different variations, expanding into accessories, or even offering services alongside your products. By diversifying your product offerings, you can capture more market share and cater to different customer needs.

- **Digital Products**: Many successful businesses expand by introducing digital products or services that complement their physical offerings. This could include e-books, online courses, membership subscriptions, or downloadable resources. Not only does this add to your revenue, but it also gives you more opportunities to scale globally.

- **Strategic Partnerships**: Look for ways to partner with other brands or influencers in your industry. These partnerships can provide new revenue streams through co-branded products, affiliate marketing, or shared customer bases. Collaborating with established businesses can also help you build credibility and expand your reach.

- **Subscription Models**: For many businesses, a subscription-based model offers consistent, predictable revenue. If your product or service has repeat value, think about how you can create a subscription service. This ensures recurring income and can also boost customer loyalty.

3. Adapt to Changing Market Trends

The market is never static, and to future-proof your business, you must remain adaptable. Consumer preferences shift, new technologies emerge, and competitors evolve. To stay relevant, your business needs to be **flexible and open to change**.

- **Continuous Innovation**: Don't rest on your laurels. Keep innovating and iterating on your product or service. This could mean introducing new features, enhancing existing ones, or exploring new ways of delivering value to your customers.

- **Monitor Industry Trends**: Stay ahead of the curve by continuously researching your industry. Subscribe to relevant blogs, attend conferences, network with other entrepreneurs, and keep an eye on emerging trends. By staying informed, you'll be able to pivot when necessary and stay relevant in the market.

- **Embrace Technology**: The future of business is undoubtedly shaped by technology. From artificial intelligence and machine learning to blockchain and the Internet of Things (IoT), technology is rapidly transforming industries. Don't shy away from adopting new technologies that can improve efficiency, customer experience, or your product offering. But remember, always evaluate if the technology aligns with your brand and adds value to your customers.

4. Building a Resilient Brand

The strength of your brand is one of the most important long-term assets you can develop. A resilient brand will withstand market fluctuations, competition, and shifts in consumer preferences. To build this, focus on the following:

- **Maintain Strong Customer Relationships**: One of the best ways to future-proof your business is by maintaining a loyal customer base. By delivering consistent value and building authentic relationships, your customers will stick with you through thick and thin. Keep engaging with them through social media, email newsletters, and customer support.

- **Invest in Customer Loyalty Programs**: Reward your customers for their loyalty through loyalty programs or personalized experiences. Giving them reasons to stay invested in your brand can turn your one-time buyers into repeat customers and brand advocates.

- **Cultivate Your Brand Values**: Your brand values will be what sets you apart from competitors. Stay true to your mission and maintain your authenticity. Consumers today are looking for brands they can trust—brands that align with their values. The more you align your product with a meaningful purpose, the more your customers will connect with you long-term.

5. Succession Planning and Leadership Development

Another key element of future-proofing your business is **succession planning**—ensuring that your company can thrive even after you're no longer involved in its daily operations. This means building a leadership team that can take the company forward.

- **Develop Internal Leadership**: Cultivate leadership skills within your organization. Encourage your employees to grow, learn, and take on more responsibility. When you build a strong leadership pipeline, you create a sustainable structure that can grow without depending solely on you.

- **Consider Your Exit Strategy**: Every entrepreneur should have an exit strategy. Whether it's selling your business, merging with another company, or handing over the reins to a new CEO, thinking ahead about how you'll exit the business can ensure that your hard work doesn't go to waste.

6. The Importance of a Long-Term Vision

Finally, always have a long-term vision for your business. Success doesn't happen overnight, and the journey of future-proofing your business takes time.

Keep your eyes on the horizon while staying grounded in the present. Understand that growth is often incremental, and the systems you put in place now will help pave the way for your long-term success. Your ability to think beyond today's success and plan for the future is what will help your business not only survive but thrive for years to come.

Book Recommendation:

For those interested in learning more about long-term business strategies and sustainability, I recommend **"Built to Last: Successful Habits of Visionary Companies" by Jim Collins and Jerry I. Porras.** This book explores the key habits and practices of companies that have endured for decades and provides actionable insights into how to build a lasting, impactful business. The strategies outlined will help you not just survive but thrive in an ever-changing market.

Conclusion: From Zero to One and Beyond

Congratulations! You've now journeyed through the 18 essential chapters designed to help you navigate the ups and downs of building a successful startup. From defining your vision and embracing failure to scaling your product and building a resilient brand, you've gained a comprehensive toolkit to help you grow a thriving business.

But here's the thing: Reading these chapters alone won't make you a successful entrepreneur. The true value comes from taking **action—starting now, with what you have**. The steps you've learned in this book are not just concepts—they are meant to be applied to your startup's journey.

Now, your next step is simple but powerful:

Take that first concrete action towards your business goal.

Here's how to do it:

1. **Start with the smallest possible step:** Whether it's validating your idea with potential customers, building your MVP, or having that first

conversation with a mentor—do something today. Break your large goals into bite-sized actions.

2. **Get comfortable with discomfort**: If you're moving out of your comfort zone, that's a good sign. Don't wait for the perfect moment; there's no such thing. Lean into the uncertainty and build momentum.

3. **Test, learn, and iterate**: Whether you succeed or fail, each outcome is valuable. Use the feedback to refine your approach, pivot if necessary, and keep iterating until you find the product-market fit.

4. **Build relationships**: As you move forward, remember that no business succeeds in isolation. Cultivate your network, build meaningful relationships with customers and mentors, and invest in your team.

5. **Commit to long-term growth**: It's easy to get caught up in the excitement of the startup world, but remember that sustainable success

comes from strategic, consistent action. Focus on building scalable systems, diversifying revenue streams, and making decisions that benefit your business not just now, but in the future.

This is where your real journey begins. Armed with the strategies, insights, and mindset shifts from this book, you're ready to make bold decisions, tackle challenges head-on, and turn your startup dream into a reality.

The next step is yours—**take it today.**

And when you're ready, remember that entrepreneurship is not a sprint. It's a marathon. Keep refining, keep learning, and keep building. The future is yours to create.

Your next step: Start now.

www.ingramcontent.com/pod-product-compliance
Lightning Source LLC
Chambersburg PA
CBHW071024240526
45469CB00006BD/2072